Presented to:

Nancy Swetnam

For faithful service

First Baptist, Granada Hills

Psalms 19:7-11

THE JESUS LIBRARY
edited by Michael Green

The Hard Sayings of Jesus
F. F. Bruce

The Teaching of Jesus
Norman Anderson

The Supremacy of Jesus
Stephen Neill

The Empty Cross of Jesus
Michael Green

The Counselling of Jesus
Duncan Buchanan

The Example of Jesus
Michael Griffiths

Jesus: Lord & Savior
F. F. Bruce

The Evidence for Jesus
R. T. France

The Healings of Jesus
Michael Harper

Jesus, Man of Prayer
Margaret Magdalen

Jesus and Power
David Prior

THE JESUS LIBRARY
Michael Green, series editor

Jesus, Man of Prayer

Margaret Magdalen

INTERVARSITY PRESS
DOWNERS GROVE, ILLINOIS 60515

Copyright © 1987 by Sister Margaret Magdalen

Published in the United States of America by InterVarsity Press, Downers Grove, Illinois, with permission from Hodder and Stoughton Limited, England.

InterVarsity Press is the book-publishing division of Inter-Varsity Christian Fellowship, a student movement active on campus at hundreds of universities, colleges and schools of nursing. For information about local and regional activities, write Public Relations Dept., InterVarsity Christian Fellowship, 6400 Schroeder Rd., P.O. Box 7895, Madison, WI 53707-7895.

Cover illustration: Janice Skivington

ISBN 0-87784-989-7
ISBN 0-87784-933-1 (The Jesus Library set)

Printed in the United States of America

Library of Congress Cataloging in Publication Data

Magdalen, Margaret, 1930-
    Jesus, man of prayer.

    (The Jesus Library)
    Includes indexes.
    1. Jesus Christ—Prayers. I. Title. II. Series.
BV229.M26 1987   232.9'5   87-26054
ISBN 0-87784-989-7

17	16	15	14	13	12	11	10	9	8	7	6	5	4	3	2	1
99	98	97	96	95	94	93	92	91	90	89	88	87				

Dedicated to
the staff and friends of St Aldate's
Church, Oxford,
with gratitude and love

EDITOR'S PREFACE

The heart of the Christian faith must always be the person of its founder. His reality, his teaching, his death, his resurrection – all of these are under frequent assault and need careful study, as other volumes in this series have provided. But part of the uniqueness of Jesus lies in his relationship of prayerful dependence on his heavenly Father. And that is an aspect of his life which is often neglected. To write such a book you need a man or woman of deep spiritual insight and profound experience in prayer. Sister Margaret Magdalen is such a person. And it is therefore with the greatest delight that I welcome her as a contributor to this series.

Sister Meg is a remarkable lady. She has been a Baptist missionary in Zaire. She has been a highly successful lecturer in a College of Education. And she has responded to the call to become an Anglican nun. We would expect something different from such a person, particularly when she is already an accomplished speaker and author. We are not disappointed: we have got something different. I do not imagine that any of us has read a book on prayer, and the prayer life of Jesus in particular, that remotely resembles this one. Sister Meg brings to the task no small understanding of the New Testament, a sensitive and biblically controlled imagination, a loyalty to scripture, a phenomenal use of the devotional literature of the ages from every strand of authentic spirituality, and a deep personal devotion to the Lord. I shall say no more. It is a remarkable book and it is written by a dear friend whom I honour and from whom I have learnt more than I can ever repay. I am sure that no reader of these pages can go away without being enriched.

Michael Green

ACKNOWLEDGMENTS

It would be impossible to name personally all those to whom I am indebted in the writing of this book, not only because they are too numerous, but because many have contributed indirectly and unknowingly through their counsel, direction and teaching over the years. Throughout the time of writing I have been conscious of the richness of the two major influences in my life – the evangelical tradition in which I was nurtured and to which I belong; and more recently, the tradition of monastic spirituality which has opened up for me hitherto unexplored country. In fact, it has been an exciting voyage of discovery as I have found the two heritages blending into a whole.

In any journey one picks up a whole wealth of impressions, information, wisdom sayings and stories. As time passes, it is not always easy to attribute the gems to their proper setting, or to recall the origins of sayings or stories. That has been my experience in writing this book. If anything has been included and unwittingly not acknowledged or traced to source, I beg forgiveness and ask you to accept this tribute to the power with which the original words must have been spoken since they have clearly lingered over many years in my memory. Please accept my gratitude for them as part of the kaleidoscope of rich things God has given me in my Christian pilgrimage and which I have sought in this book to share.

There are some, however, to whom I wish to express particular thanks for their support and help in this venture. To Sylvia and John Barrow for their generous hospitality and unfailing kindness. Much of this book has been written under their roof. To Gwenda Hutchinson and Ann Morgan of

Shefford Office Services for the proficient skill with which they typed the scripts, and their friendly and ever-cheerful service. To the Reverend Basil Davies (Chaplain of Community of St Mary the Virgin) for kindly reading the manuscript and offering advice and encouragement. To Edward England and Michael Green from whom the invitation to write came, for confident assurances which launched me into the project. To the Sisters of my Community who have given particular practical help especially – Sister Mildred Rebecca, Sister Olive Frances, Sister Hilda Verity, Sister Isobel Joy, Sister Barbara Claire, Sister Rozalja and Oblate Jane Richards; and those who would not wish to be named but who have specially covered the whole enterprise with prayer.

I am greatly indebted to Sister Martha CP and the Calvary Sisters of Moreneng, Gaborone, Botswana, for their generous hospitality in providing a refuge to write during the final stages of rewriting and correcting, and to Elisabeth Pearce of St Hugh's College, Oxford, for typing the final three chapters.

AUTHOR'S PREFACE

It took a long time to agree to tackle this book. Who would not have trembled to write on such a subject!

The qualms were justified for, from the moment I began to write, the spiritual onslaught began. It is only in retrospect that I can see and feel something of the inwardly rewarding experience it has been to tiptoe day after day into the presence of the praying Christ, through the scriptures, through silence and personal reflection, there to discover things I never knew before. Through these weeks, the measure of the stature of his fullness has become increasingly vivid.

I knew from the outset that I could not write a scholarly book, nor was that my brief. In imagination, my readers have been those of my friends who are mothers and housewives, busy professional people whose work consumes most of their day-to-day energy but who want and need spiritual input and nourishment in their Christian pilgrimage. This book, therefore, is devotional reading, not without its demands, but in the nature of a conversation – a sharing with those who also long to discover something of the Lord's path of prayer.

It seemed right to try and apply something of what we learn of Jesus' practice of prayer in our own lives, so where it has seemed appropriate, I have included, in the Appendix, some practical suggestions related to particular chapters.

The biblical quotations are, unless otherwise stated, from the Revised Standard Version, and the Psalms from D. L. Frost, J. A. Emerton and A. A. Macintosh, *The Psalms. A New Translation for Worship* (Collins 1977), whose verse numbers occasionally differ from other translations and which I designate as NTW in the text.

Throughout I have sought to ground the discussion in biblical teaching, but at the same time I have tried to draw on the wisdom of the devotional masters and spiritual classics of all ages. The biographical dictionary of authors will, hopefully, enable readers to place the author in his/her right century and cultural background. I am indebted to F. L. Cross and E. A. Livingstone (eds), *The Oxford Dictionary of the Christian Church* (OUP, 1974) and G. S. Wakefield (ed), *A Dictionary of Christian Spirituality* (SCM, 1983) for helpful information in this.

Margaret Magdalen CSMV
Wantage, April 1986

INTRODUCTION:

A PORTRAIT OF JESUS – the man of prayer

The path of prayer thyself hast trod
Lord teach us how to pray.

Most of us find it helpful when we begin a jigsaw to have
before us a picture of the puzzle we are about to try and piece
together. In the same way, this portrait is offered as an
overview – a cameo-sized composite picture – of Jesus the
man of prayer. In the following chapters, the picture will be
broken down into smaller 'pieces' and each one examined
more closely.

It is holy ground on which we walk, and we need to tread
with utmost reverence. It is a delicate and awesome thing to
share the secrets of *anyone's* prayer life. Indeed, it would be
downright intrusive unless it were at their invitation, and even
then the greatest sensitivity and humility are needed. How
much more, then, the Lord's life of prayer!

There was obviously something very special about the
prayer life of Jesus that led the disciples to say, 'Lord, teach us
to pray.' What he taught them and what they have recorded
for us of his own practice have been left for us as the clues he
invites and intends us to pick up, ponder, share and appropriate in our own path of prayer. For, 'prayer in Christ on earth
and in us cannot be two different things'.[1] Through them we
come to see Jesus the mystic, Jesus the contemplative, Jesus
the intercessor, Jesus the faithful son of Abraham, recipient
of the Hebrew scriptures and liturgy of his faith, Jesus who
wept in prayer and cried out in bewilderment to his Father,

Jesus who prayed redemptively through the unquenchable, unconquerable love that flowed from him towards those who hated him. Jesus who committed himself utterly to his Father and whose ceaseless aspiration was to glorify him.

It encourages us to learn something of the practical aspects of his prayer—where and when he chose to pray, the occasions on which he needed and delighted to pray, the forms of prayer he used, the intimate address with which he spoke to his Father and invited his followers to do the same. He shows us that prayer is not knowing *about* God, but knowing God.

It is a consolation to know that he too experienced testing, darkness and dereliction in prayer, that the greatest experiences of his life took place while he prayed, that the crisis events were preceded or followed by prayer.

We see that at times he needed to be alone in prayer; at others he sought company — and felt badly let down when those chosen to 'watch and pray' with him fell asleep.

It becomes clear that despite the enormous pressures on his time and energy, he did not, indeed *could* not, allow prayer to become a casualty. Communion with his Father was the mainspring of his life. His bodily senses led him into wonder and contemplation. His work was an offering of prayer. His healing ministry was a way of praying — restoring the joy of wholeness to those broken in body, mind or spirit. His teaching was prayer leading men to reality and truth. His forgiving was prayer bringing men into right relationship with God and themselves. His denunciations were a form of prayer sweeping aside masks and illusions and exposing the truth. His compassion was prayer, for it allowed people to see themselves through his eyes and to come to truthful self-knowledge. He himself was the way, the truth and the life, and every encounter, every relationship, became prayer.

Some years ago, Alan Ecclestone wrote a book entitled, *Yes to God.*[2] Jesus, himself, was a living 'Yes' to God — the 'Yes' of perfect obedience, the 'Yes' of divine sonship, the 'Yes' of a will that willed one will with the Father. The words of Richard Rolle perhaps echo the response of Jesus himself:

'All my desires are one desire and that for nought but Thee.'[3]

It was his greatest and most complete prayer that he uttered in the words 'Thy will be done,' which has been called 'the pure prayer of love'.[4] It was not only the culmination of his life, prayed in his last agony, it was his ceaseless aspiration throughout life.

As we observe the praying Christ in these pages, we have of necessity to look at some of his teaching on prayer as well as his example. We need to linger reflectively over something of the inner meaning of the specific prayer he gave to his disciples. Any such study must surely quicken our desire to pray and increase our sense of urgency about this aspect of our Christian discipleship. As Andrew Murray wrote, 'Christ's life and work, his suffering and death – it was all prayer, all dependence on God, trust in God, receiving from God, surrender to God. Thy redemption, O believer, is a redemption wrought out by prayer and intercession: *thy Christ is a praying Christ.*'[5]

One thing emerges with outstanding clarity as we focus reverent attention on Jesus the man of prayer: 'He did not say prayers some of the time. He *was* prayer all of the time.'[6] As temples of his Holy Spirit he continues to pray in and through us.

'The life he lived for thee, the life he lives in thee, is a praying life . . .'[7]

A prayer

The Lord Jesus Himself will teach you
how you should pray.
He is the creative word
which you may receive in the silence of your
heart
and the fruitful soil of your life.
Listen attentively to what He will say;
be swift to carry out
what He will ask of you.

You have been promised His Spirit
who will bear your poor little efforts
before the throne of grace
and into the intimacy of the Living God . . .
Your prayer will take countless forms
because it is the echo of your life,
and a reflection of the inexhaustible light
in which God dwells.[8]

1
'CONSIDER THE LILIES' – praying through the senses

Consider the lilies of the field, how they grow; they neither toil nor spin; yet I tell you, even Solomon in all his glory was not arrayed like one of these . . . if God so clothes the grass of the field . . . will he not much more clothe you, O men of little faith?

(Matt 6:28–30)

When and how did Jesus learn to pray? Above all others, Mary must have influenced his early spiritual development in a unique way. The bonding from birth between mother and son would have enveloped him in the atmosphere of prayer in which she lived. Albeit unconsciously, he must have picked up something of her attentive stillness as she pondered things in her heart. Now that we know, through modern research, far more about 'the secret life of the unborn child'[1] and just how acutely the foetus in the womb is affected by the disposition and moods of the mother, her own fears and anxieties, or as in Mary's case, her purity of heart and sure trust in God, we can understand more fully the profound responsibility given to her when God chose to ask her to become the temple of his incarnate Son . . . and she chose to say 'Yes.'[2]

Joseph, too, would have had an important role in the life of the growing Jesus for, as head of the household and in line with Jewish custom, it would have been his responsibility to teach the child his first official prayers – the liturgical prayers which would form the foundation of his lifelong devotional pattern. From Joseph, Jesus would have received his pre-school training. To Joseph it would have fallen to take him to the synagogue and hand him on to the rabbi for instruction. And in those out-of-school hours, what bond was built up between Joseph the carpenter and his devoted apprentice?

Yet there was a further 'teacher' in Christ's early spiritual life – his senses. Perhaps it was through them that Jesus offered his first spontaneous prayer.

Wonder

Have you ever watched a small child studying the movements of an insect, or touching a sticky bud for the first time, or listening to a sea-shell? Have you ever seen a group of youngsters crouched round a rock pool, silent, attentive, intrigued, totally absorbed and full of wonder?

Silent wonder is actually their first, very simple and natural prayer. It was your first prayer and mine, though we have forgotten it and wouldn't have recognised it as such at the time. It was our natural response to mystery. The child Jesus would most likely have begun that area of his prayer life where other children begin – with mystery and wonder.

Children have a tremendous capacity for wonder. In that respect, they are natural contemplatives, for it is an essential ingredient of contemplation. In childhood, and indeed as adults, the senses often become doors into wonder. Evelyn Underhill exhorted us to begin with that first form of contemplation which the old mystics sometimes called the 'discovery of God in his creatures'.[3]

Obviously, our surroundings largely determine what impressions and information our senses will receive. As a country boy, in all probability free to roam the hills of Galilee, Jesus would have developed the countryman's keen ear and quick eye. By the time he was a man, he clearly had an intense interest in the natural world and his teaching gave the clue not only to what he saw, heard and felt, but to how he reflected on what he had received through his senses. He who could speak of the wind that 'blows where it wills' (John 3:8) had clearly revelled in this marvellous and unpredictable element, and in the sun and rain too, which fall without discrimination on the unrighteous as well as the righteous (Matt 5:45). Judging by the number of references to wildlife (the foxes, wolves, dogs, birds and fish) as well as the not-so-wild (ewes, lambs, swine), animals must have fascinated him, and perhaps he them, for holiness produces a strange affinity with animals. We can imagine his intelligent, young eyes gathering up what he observed and storing it away as a resource for consideration, enjoyment and reflection. If *we* have the ability to recall memories at will, and re-member our fragmented experiences into a cohesive whole as a way of savouring life more fully and recovering spiritual energy, we cannot believe that he who was so attuned to his Father through involvement in the natural world would do less. He grew up with that earthy wisdom that belongs to those who live close to the soil. Sensitive to sights and sounds, tones and textures, and able to read something of their hidden meaning, his world must have been one of constant delight, surprise and wonder.

Contemplation

Contemplation is not, as people often mistakenly believe, chiefly a matter of advanced techniques in prayer, a secret knowledge of mysteries, higher states of awareness accompanied by visions, ecstasies and levitation. It is primarily a way of looking and listening, of beholding, marvelling, considering. It moves on into the depths of the will, sometimes in great darkness and aridity, but it often begins with wonder. In one sense, we are all called to contemplation; and if children in general are natural contemplatives, surely the boy Jesus would have been particularly so with his hypersensitivity and extraordinary powers of perception. For those qualities which were so apparent in the adult Jesus must have grown from 'mustard seed' beginnings in infancy to the full flowering in manhood.

As adults, most of us have lost the ability to bow before the mysteries of life. Driven by a compulsive urge to explain and rationalise everything, and beset by so many cares and responsibilities, we are unable to lose ourselves utterly, as a child does when he is totally absorbed in whatever has captured his interest. We find it almost impossible to give our undivided attention to anything because we are too distracted (literally, 'pulled apart') by conflicting demands and interests; so dissipated by the multiplicity of claims upon our time and energy.

Becoming as children

No wonder Jesus exhorted his followers to become childlike! He doubtless knew that part of that 'becoming' would lead to the recovery of the art of losing oneself in wonder, love and praise. In this the child is closer to the kingdom than adults, for prayer has remained the simple thing that basically it should be. Michel Quoist puts it very beautifully:

> God says: I like youngsters. I want people to be like them.
> I don't like old people unless they are still children.
> I want only children in my kingdom; this has been decreed
>   from the beginning of time . . .
>
> But above all, I like youngsters because of the look in
>   their eyes. In their eyes I can read their age.
> In my heaven, there will be only five-year-old eyes, for I
>   know of nothing more beautiful than the pure eyes of a
>   child.
> It is not surprising, for I live in children, and it is I who
>   look out through their eyes.[4]

This childlike art of absorption, which most adults have sacrified in the 'muchness and manyness'[5] of life, Jesus seemed able to retain even in maturity. He was able to give his *full* attention to people, to be singleminded and simple. How else could he have spoken of the need for a 'single eye' (cf. Matt 6:22)?

Do not be anxious

Part of the reason why children are able to lose themselves in a game or story is that they are normally carefree and without anxiety. They are content to trust adults to shoulder burdens beyond their capacity. Thus they are free to get on with the business of living, to throw themselves into the particular interest of the present moment. They do, of course, anticipate things ahead and look back on memorable events. But they are not usually weighed down by fears about the future or tormented by events of the past. *Now* is what matters, unless, like the children of Dickens' novels or the victims of present-day child-abuse, circumstances have forced them to carry adult burdens prematurely.

That childlike gift of abandonment comes from trust; and trust, like wonder, is essential to contemplative prayer. We can hardly be still, receptive, totally absorbed in God, if inwardly we are churned up by worry, if the pull of past or future is tearing us apart.

It was in the context of his teaching about anxiety that Jesus told his disciples to 'consider the lilies' – to observe their growth. But it is teaching related to prayer. The disciples are invited to consider, to notice, to learn from the lilies, not by a peremptory glance but by a long, feasting look. 'Consider' has about it the feeling of restful reflection, leisurely appreciation, a freedom of heart to gaze and wonder, and, in doing so, to discover truth. This kind of looking has to be for its own sake, not for any end-product; not with our greedy consumer-society tendency to do something with half an eye on what we can get out of it.

In considering the lilies, which obviously Jesus must have done himself, the disciples would discover a truth not only about trust but, even more, about living provisionally – that is, as those for whom provision has been made. They were bidden to ponder the carefree existence of this humble meadow flower that does nothing to earn the right to live, nothing to provide for its present or future needs, nothing to impress, nothing to flourish more effectively or proliferate more abundantly. More beautiful than any ornate royal robe, the lily is simply as God intended it to be – itself . . . without pretence or pride, without anxiety or neuroses, without toiling or spinning.

And not only the lily! More astounding still was the short-lived grass of the field – of so little worth it was commonly used as a form of cheap fuel. There in the field one day and gone the next! Yet each seemingly unimportant blade was provided with the protective clothing of a delicate membrane.

Sparrows, too, were reckoned of little worth – two could be sold for a farthing. Yet no sparrow, or any other bird for that matter, would fall to the ground, injured or dead, without the creator being aware. (It was a happy choice to speak of the humble sparrow, for even city dwellers have a chance of 'considering' this ubiquitous little creature.)

Jesus singled out for special attention these ordinary, rather despised, parts of creation on which no one placed any value – field flowers, grass, sparrows – which could neverthe-less become gateways to contemplation. These were to be the icons through which the disciples would penetrate the mys-tery of God's providence and protection, and discover hidden wisdom and truth about God's relationship with his creation. And they would do so by using the eyes of the body and the eyes of understanding. As Mother Julian of Norwich says: 'Truth sees God: wisdom gazes on God. And these two produce a third, a holy, wondering delight in God, which is love. Where there is indeed truth and wisdom, there too is love, springing from them both.'[6]

The out-of-doors was always an important praying place for Jesus. It was God's atmosphere where he breathed freely and in which he could be alone. It gave a spaciousness to his spiritual life, deepened his understanding of his Father and evoked awe. It provided the context of many of his deepest spiritual experiences – the river and the desert, the mountains and the hills, a lake and a garden, the road to Jerusalem and the road to Emmaus. Much of his teaching was given in the open air and many of his miracles performed there. And, of course, the years of his peripatetic ministry were mostly lived out of doors in tough and demanding conditions. The animals might be able to retire to their natural habitats at night, but he often had nowhere to provide him with creaturely security, nothing to satisfy his natural homing instinct. 'Are you prepared for that?' he had to ask one ardent, would-be follower.

The outcome of prayer of the senses

Jesus was a man who studied nature by paying attention to it, whose careful and prayerful observation of it formed a springboard to contemplation. The fruit of that prayer is revealed in his teaching, where agriculture and sheep farming, animal and plant life, reeds of the desert and hairs of the human head, fruit and fish, sun and rain, wind and floods, salt and light, weather signals of the sky by day and stars by night all become the means of apprehending divine truth.

The parables may possibly have been spontaneous stories, but it is far more likely they were born of much reflection in the hours spent alone in prayer. The things of the natural world, seen, heard, touched and savoured through the senses, became the substance of some of the fiercest attacks (e.g. against the Pharisees) which Jesus launched in his teaching about the kingdom.

A. M. Hunter has said that we misunderstand the Galilean ministry of Jesus if 'we picture it *only* as a peaceful pastoral wherein the serene wisdom of the Teacher accorded well with the flowers and birds of Galilee. Such a picture we obtain only if we scale down the miracles, interpret the parables as charming stories about moral commonplaces, and evacuate the eschatological sayings of their mystery and depth.' We ought to picture this part of Jesus' ministry 'dynamically, not statically, and polemically rather than pastorally'.[7]

The parables (as J. Jeremias has said) are 'weapons of war'

wielded by Jesus with urgency at a time of crisis. So, far from being 'a high-souled teacher patiently indoctrinating the multitudes with truths of timeless wisdom', he is rather to be seen as 'the strong Son of God, armed with his Father's power, spear-heading the attack against the devil and all his works, and calling men to decide on whose side of the battle they will be'.[8] This removes any suggestion that Jesus idealised the things of nature. He was deeply influenced by his environment, but not reduced to maudlin sentimentality.

The senses and the city

It would be a grave distortion, and a sad discouragement to those living in the inner city, if we saw only the beauties of nature as the Lord's contemplative material. It might have formed a good deal of it since most of his life was spent in rural districts, but by no means all of it. To those who live in urban areas it might be that he would say, 'You neglect your senses to your cost. In silence you can rediscover them. A silent, prayerful walk will teach you as "much about inner cities as countryside"[9].'

How did he experience the city himself and relate it to his prayer?

'And when he drew near and saw the city he wept over it . . .' (Luke 19:41). These were surely not the impulsive tears of a fleeting pang of regret. When he drew near, would he not have paused and looked . . . considered and pondered? With the looking came a great longing, 'Would that even today you knew the things that make for peace' (Luke 19:42). Then he wept as he saw and understood to what tragic consequences the blindness of the Jews would lead. Looking, longing and weeping all have their place in prayer.

Again, the Lord's deep love of the city is expressed powerfully in his lament over Jerusalem: 'O Jerusalem, Jerusalem, killing the prophets and stoning those who are sent to you! How often would I have gathered your children together as a hen gathers her brood under her wings, and you would not! Behold, your house is forsaken' (Luke 13:34,35a).

His anguish in both these cases *was* his prayer.

Would that more of us looked and longed, wept and prayed over our cities; would that more often we took the harsh and ugly things that we see and hear, the squalor and dehumanisation that we meet, and allowed them to be icons[10] by which we are drawn into the mystery of the suffering God who 'specialises in transfiguration'.[11]

It was the sight of squalor, the smell of opium dens, the sound of dogs being flayed alive that provided the background and impetus to Jackie Pullinger's prayer walks around the Walled City of Hong Kong.[12]

We do not lack for petitionary material in our Western cities – be they affluent or poor, ancient or industrial – if we have the sensitive awareness of prayerful observation. Such travailing is strategic prayer, an identification in prayer with Christ who 'always lives to make intercession' (Heb 7:25) for London and New York, Belfast and Beirut. Speaking of Beirut, a man from that city commented about prayer:

the difficulty [about the Middle East] . . . is that words have lost their meaning. For instance, if you mention hope, you might as well be talking about despair for all the effect it has on people. Therefore I would talk mostly of waiting upon God and quietly searching for his presence. Real prayer is offering what you can see and grasping what is happening, however painful and beastly it is, and waiting on God with it, almost as though you have it in your hands.[13]

That seems to sum up, in modern idiom, how Jesus prayed for the city.

The senses and the desert

Nor, of course, would Jesus have found the desert altogether congenial to his senses. The extremes of heat and cold, the glare of the sun, the merciless winds and the great void all make the wilderness an inhospitable place. The vast silence and solitude of the desert may indeed at times be conducive to prayer. They beckon appealingly to one willing for a life of presence to the desert and presence to God. But the desert is also the place of struggle and testing, the place where we are simplified and stripped of our 'excess baggage' – the non-essentials that hinder mobility and threaten safety in the journey from oasis to oasis. And that stripping often hurts. It is the place of temptation. The people of God discovered this and were defeated. Jesus experienced it and conquered. A long succession of holy men and women have followed him into the desert-place precisely to enter into conflict with the Evil One, to engage in spiritual warfare in a particularly direct way, experiencing the darker side of the desert as they do so.

'On one of my trips', says William Johnston, 'I became acutely aware of the diabolical dimension of the great and terrible wilderness. Whereas Jerusalem is filled with places of worship, the desert south of 'En Gedi seemed not only empty but profoundly godless.'[14]

It was to this godless environment that the Holy Spirit *drove* Jesus for an extended time of prayer as he listened and discerned God's ways for the mission entrusted to him.

Prayer and fasting

The aspect of Christ's prayer which went with his desert experiences was fasting. We are told specifically of the lengthy fast in the desert after his baptism (Matt 4:2), but his instructions to his disciples included a number of references which suggest it was a regular part of his devotional practice.

The disciples are not to advertise their fasting in order to receive the acclaim of men (Matt 6:16–18). (NB: Jesus said, 'When you fast . . .', not '*If* you fast . . .' It is *assumed* that they will!) Spiritual power cannot flow in and through them without this discipline. Answering their query as to why they had not been able to heal the epileptic boy, Jesus said, 'this kind never comes out except by prayer and fasting' (Matt 17:21). The Pharisees levelled a criticism at Jesus because he did not insist on stricter fasting among his disciples (Mark 2:18). The proud Pharisee who arrogantly claimed that he was 'not like other men', reminded God that he fasted 'twice a week' (Luke 18:12). Evidently that was unusually ascetic – or at least the Pharisee himself considered it noteworthy.

Every Jew would, of course, have been familiar with the practice of fasting from his own religious practice and from knowledge of the scriptures. Fasting in the Old Testament is linked with penitence (Ps 35:13; 69:10), with bereavement (2 Sam 12:23), with national mourning (Neh 9:1; Esther 4:3), with intercession in a crisis (Dan 6:18; Joel 2:12).

For Jesus it was linked with discerning God's will, receiving God's power and awaiting the consummation of God's kingdom. (It was after the ascension that the disciples resumed their fasting – that is, in the interim between the inauguration of the kingdom and its expected fulfilment [cf. Acts 13:2,3].)

The motive for fasting had to be right – the outward act alone would be valueless. It was not to be used as a way of impressing God or other men, nor as an attempt to manipulate God, somehow putting him under an obligation because of the act of self-denial. In the days of Zechariah God asked his people, 'When you fasted and mourned . . . was it for me that you fasted? And when you eat and drink, do you not eat for yourselves and drink for yourselves?' (Zech 7:5,6). He told Zechariah to say to the people that he would far rather that they rendered true judgment, showed kindness and mercy, cared about the oppressed, the alienated, the deprived and were generally willing to listen to him, than that they bothered about fasting. Fasting has no meaning if it is inconsistent with the rest of one's life. It cannot be used as a make-weight in an impoverished spiritual life or as a way of masking hypocrisy. In Isaiah 58:3 we read the complaint of God's people, 'Why have we fasted, and thou seest it not?' And the Lord's answer – 'Fasting like yours this day will not make your voice to be heard on high. Is such the fast that I choose . . . ? Is not this the fast that I choose: to loose the bonds of wickedness, to undo the thongs of the yoke, to let the oppressed go free . . . ? Is it not to share your bread with the hungry, and bring the homeless poor into your house; when you see the naked to cover him . . . ?' (Isa 58:4b,5a,6–7).

No wonder the church includes these words in its Lenten liturgy as a salutary recall to God's priorities, a reminder that fasting is primarily *for* not *from*; *for* God not only *from* food. John Wesley said: 'Let [fasting] be done unto the Lord with our eye singly fixed on him. Let our intention herein be this, and this alone, to glorify our Father which is in heaven.'[15]

Why then, if fasting deepens the quality of spiritual life and attunes the inner ear to hear God's voice, did Jesus apparently sit loose to it where his disciples were concerned? Had the Pharisees actually got a point?

The striking thing which emerges from this exchange between Jesus and his critics (cf. Mark 2:18–20) is the connection between fasting and feasting. His followers were only to fast when they had first learnt to feast. Those who have recognised, welcomed and feasted with the bridegroom (cf. Matt 25:6) may appropriately fast during his absence as they await his return and the celebration of the 'Lamb's high banquet'.

There are many reasons for fasting. It is a discipline known and practised by adherents of practically every other faith – and far more rigorously than most Christians! For Jesus, fasting was linked inseparably with prayer. It has continued to be so in the Christian tradition. It is enjoined, not to induce mystical states, nor simply to gain mastery of the body and its appetites, but to bring us to a new freedom in prayer.

We need to note in passing that for Jesus fasting was no easier than it is for any other human being. His hunger was real. Doubtless he went through the normal progression from acute hunger, headaches, dizziness and sleepiness to the stage of wide-awakeness, discernment and clarity of vision. He was tempted to turn stones into bread not just to feed the poor but to satisfy the probable pangs that gnawed away inside him in the early days of the fast. At this point, it is a temptation to give up in any attempt to fast. The stomach seems to shriek for food. A dietician once described fasting as 'the punctuation marks in my relationship with food'.[16] In the initial stages the body is ridding itself of all the toxic matter that has been poisoning the system. With mind and body purged, and with an interior hollowness created by silence and solitude as a receptive space for God, we find ourselves on the threshold of adoration and worship, as Anna did (Luke 2:37); our perceptions are cleansed and there lies before us a landscape where everything is seen in sharp focus.

Misuse of the senses

In earlier times, some teachers of spirituality sought to eliminate from life and worship all that might be pleasing to the senses. Somehow, it was thought faintly wicked to enjoy beauty in whatever guise. Yet nothing could be further from the attitude of Jesus who used his senses to *engage* with the created world in its varied aspects.

Obviously the senses, if misused, can become a hindrance to prayer. They can draw us away rather than lead *to* God. The eyes that behold his glory in creation can also covet and lust; the lips that sing God's praises can also lie; the hands held out to receive him in bread and wine can also be cruel, dishonest and lazy; the ears that have been tuned in to the courts of heaven can listen to gossip and critical destruction of another; the tongue that has tasted heavenly food can be the cause of untold damage; the noses that have revelled in the fragrance of flowers and aromatic spices can permit a seductive perfume to lead to lust of the heart.

The church fathers were right, of course, to emphasise the need for guarding the senses. But control is very different from suppression. That is no answer. Sanctification is. The senses can serve both 'angels and dirt'.[17] Rather than rejecting them we need to permit them the angelic role:

If only we knew how to look at life as God sees it,
    we should realize that nothing is secular in the world,

but that everything contributes to the building of the
   kingdom
of God. To have faith is not only to raise
one's eyes to God to contemplate him; it is also to look at
this world – but with Christ's eyes . . .
We must pray to have sufficient faith to know how to look
   at life[18]

It has been said that 'if the doors of our perception were
cleansed, we should see everything as it really is – holy'.[19]
That is how Jesus saw. That is how he looked round upon
creation and found that everything that God had made was
'very good' (Gen 1:31). As we develop 'inner eyes' and allow
Christ to penetrate our whole being, the world will no longer
be an obstacle; indeed, we shall often find ourselves saying
with awe, 'Surely the Lord is in this place; and I did not know
it' (Gen 28:16). He is ever seeking to manifest himself in
ordinary ways, and natural things begin to take on for us a
new vibrant quality.

It marks a growth in prayer – this new sense of the reality
and beauty of God in his world. 'The life of God sings in his
creation,' said Thomas Merton. 'Let me seek, then, the gift of
silence, and poverty, and solitude, where everything I touch is
turned to prayer: where the sky is my prayer, the birds are my
prayer, the wind in the trees is my prayer, for God is all in
all.'[20]

It leads to an affinity with creation, as Richard Jefferies
testifies:

Dreary in appearance, I am breathing full of existence; I
was aware of the grassblades, the flowers, the leaves on the
hawthorn and trees. I seemed to live more largely through
them, as if each were a pore through which I drank. The
grasshoppers called and leaped, the greenfinches sang, the
blackbirds happily fluted, all the air hummed with life. I
was plunged deep in existence, and with all that existence I
prayed. Through every grass blade in the thousand,
thousand grasses; through the million leaves, veined and

edge-cut, on bush and tree; through the song-notes and the marked feathers of the birds; through the insects' hum and the colour of the butterflies; through the soft warm air, the flecks of clouds dissolving – I used them all for prayer . . . All the glory of the sunrise filled me with broader and furnace-like vehemence of prayer.[21]

This is no mere pantheism, but evidence of a deepening relationship with him who is 'the first-born of all creation', for whom all things were created and in whom 'all things hold together' (Col 1:15,17).

Jesus knew how to look at life. He was able to find God in earth and sky and sea, in city and temple, in the home and in the desert. But he also found him in the hungry, the thirsty, the naked, the imprisoned (cf. Matt 25:34–40). Today he would expect us, if we have learnt how to look at life as God sees it, to find him in the urban priority areas, the streets of Calcutta, the relief camps of Ethiopia and the rubbish dumps of Latin America with their scavenging population.

Finding God in all things

In fact, if we know how to look at life, we shall, as St Ignatius taught, 'find God in all things'.[22] He spoke not simply of the beauties of nature or of man-made creations, but of experiences and circumstances, of the wider sphere of contemporary affairs, of relationships, work, leisure, disappointments, brokenness – some of which might, on the surface of things, seem more calculated to reveal evil than God, but the seeing eye will find God in the unexpected. Jesus himself certainly found God in the 'common things of life, its goings out and in . . . in each duty and each deed, however small and mean'.[23] Heavenly wisdom was rooted in earthly reality. Prayer did not lead him into the realm of philosophical thought, ideas and abstract concepts, but into the material. It was the lost coin of a woman's headpiece (Luke 15:8), lamps under bushels (Mark 4:21), children piping and dancing in the village square

(Matt 11:17), badly patched garments (Mark 2:21), or burst wine skins (Mark 2:22), that became the substance of his reflection. The domestic details, far from being divorced from prayer, reinforced for him spiritual truths.

His was no 'feet-off-the-ground spirituality'[24] but one which touched-down on human experience in every area of life. He was able to find God in the concrete reality of daily living.

Teilhard de Chardin has said of our relationship to God:

> God, in all that is most living and incarnate in Him, is not far away from us, altogether apart from the world we see, touch, hear, smell and taste about us. Rather He awaits us every instant in our action, in the work of the moment . . . He is at the tip of my pen, my brush, my needle – of my heart and of my thought.[25]

Part of those hidden years of preparation in Nazareth had been for Jesus a learning to hallow natural things by his relationship to them. For him it was not the pen, the brush or the needle, but the saw, the plane and the hammer.

In his Rule, St Benedict has a deeply sacramental understanding of the whole of life. He would not countenance any division between the sacred and secular. Moments of vision had to be balanced and worked out in the humdrum affairs of every day. God may be found as much in work as in worship. The kitchen utensils were as sacred as the vessels of the altar. There are echoes here of Brother Lawrence caught up in contemplation in the midst of his pots and pans and the kitchen sink!

In her study of the Rule of St Benedict, Esther de Waal says:

> Seeking God does not demand the unusual, the spectacular, the heroic. It asks of me as wife, mother, housewife that I do the most ordinary, often dreary and humdrum things that face me each day, with a loving openness that will allow them to become my own immediate way to God.[26]

We may not feel we can reach dizzy heights in prayer, but we can all do ordinary things well – with attention and single-mindedness. That prepares the ground for prayer. It teaches us how to become absorbed, so that when we come to those periods specifically set aside for prayer we are half way there already.

Jesus' prayer life did not begin and end on the hillsides considering lilies and birds. It evolved in the workshop as he gave his mind to the task in hand. 'Mindfulness', they call it in the East.

Bishop Peter Ball of Lewes was passing through the kitchen one day while some of his youthful household were peeling potatoes. Looking over their shoulders he said gently, 'You'll never make contemplatives!' They weren't concentrating on their job – the eyes had not been removed.

Of course we can idealise and exaggerate the relationship between work and prayer, and 'finding God in all things' does not mean that we shall always be *immediately* conscious of our discovery. It will become clear to us as we reflect on experience, savour it, allow it to yield its full richness. Most of us live life at too superficial a level and 'superficiality is the curse of our age'.[27]

Jesus experienced life at depth – which is not the same as being overly intense and earnest.

We know that he used the prayer of touch in the carpenter's shop. His sensitive fingers would, surely, run along a piece of wood assessing its potential, appreciating and exploring its possibilities. They would detect the merest roughness, the smallest notch. No yoke left his shop that would be anything but 'easy' for the animal to wear (Matt 11:30). The frames for carrying loads would be made of the lightest wood in order not to add unnecessarily to the beast's burden. Everything would be well done with full, loving attention and proper pride. Eyes and hands, sight and touch would combine to glorify his Father. And such an attitude to work brings reverence for the tools that we use and a proper respect for their function. *Things* matter as well as people and need to be handled gently and carefully. For they, too, have been created and therefore reflect the creator's richness of resource.

Every item made by Jesus at the carpenter's bench would have carried prayerful attention to detail and finish as he thought of those who would buy and use his handiwork. Did he come to reverence the wood and the nails that he handled as the tools of his trade? Could he ever have had any intuition that, materially speaking, these would be the very instruments by which he would die?

The open air and the beauties of creation provide for many of us the best ethos for re-educating our senses and recovering the childlike 'vision deadened or destroyed by the careful expectations of most modern schools (and parents)'.[28] But equally, the place where our awakened senses will most frequently lead us to prayer is the place of our work. It is in the car we service, the letter we type, the bread which we make that we shall find God. For Jesus, praying through his sense of touch was not reserved for 'holy' work. The fingers that made clay and gently touched the eyes of the blind, the hand that raised up a little girl from the sleep of death, those that touched the lepers, were the same which in the workshop had been trained to do 'all things well' (Mark 7:37).

Prayer of the senses makes a unity of life, drawing together the menial tasks and the uplifting moments of reflection. Far from disengaging ourselves from the world, we are brought into closer touch with it.

'A man may only detach himself from nature in order to revert to it again and, in hallowed contact with it, find his way to God,' said Martin Buber.

There is nothing in the world which does not point a way to the fear of God and the service of God . . . By no means can it be our true task, in the world in which we have been set, to turn away from the things and beings which we meet on our way and that attract our hearts; our task is precisely to get in touch, by hallowing our relationship with them, with what manifests itself as beauty, pleasure and enjoyment

. . . Rejoicing in the world, if we hallow it with our whole being, leads to rejoicing in God.[29]

This was the Hasidic tradition in which Jesus grew up. This is what he would have been taught by his rabbi. In turn, he invites us to hallow creation by our lives, to enter into this tradition of his people by 'considering' the lilies, the grass, the sparrows, the foundations of buildings, moths and rust, pearls and pigs, roads and gates, bread and fish, wolves and sheep, water and wine, and to let the wonder that is born of that reflection turn us into five-year-olds for whom there is a welcome in his kingdom.

> Let him who seeks
> rest not until he find.
> For finding
> he shall wonder.
> And wondering he shall enter
> The Kingdom,
> and in the Kingdom he shall rest.[30]

If we need any further persuasion that Jesus himself allowed his senses to assist him in prayer, and intended us to do so too, we have only to remember his dying legacy.

Using, as so often before, material things to convey spiritual power, he took bread, blessed and broke it. He poured out wine. He touched, handled and tasted these homely things and gave them to his disciples to receive bodily so that they might be nourished spiritually.

How well he understood the human need for symbols.

When faith exists as a struggle to believe in spite of empirical and temperamental pressure to unbelief, when the whole life of feeling is dead, when nothing is left but stark loyalty to God as He is dimly and waveringly apprehended to be – then the sheer objectivity, even the express materialism, of a sacrament gives it a value that nothing else can have.[31]

'The life of God sings in his creation' and the life of God flows through our bodies, and we apprehend it in both cases through our senses. 'To be holy is not to be heavenly but to know God in one's earthiness and in one's flesh.'[32]

The senses, however, are not an end in themselves in prayer, only the means to an end – just as the senses in loving are only *one* of the stepping stones to deeper loving.

As we look forward to the time when spiritual realities will no longer need to be communicated through the veil of sacraments and symbols, so having led us by many paths into the presence of God, our senses will recede into the background of prayer. Their work will be done.

We shall be immersed in 'the silence of eternity' which is 'interpreted by love',[33] there to behold and see, to consider and contemplate, the glory of the Lord.

For leaving behind everything that is observed, not only what sense comprehends but also what the intelligence thinks it sees, it keeps on penetrating deeper until by the intelligence's yearning for understanding it gains access to the invisible and the incomprehensible, and there it sees God. This is the true knowledge of what is sought; this is the seeing that consists in not seeing, because that which is sought transcends all knowledge . . .[34]

(See the Appendix for practical follow-up suggestions.)

2

'TO A LONELY PLACE' – praying in solitude and silence

And in the morning, a great while before day, he rose and went out to a lonely place, and there he prayed.

(Mark 1:35)

Why did Jesus seek the solitude of lonely places in the early morning or during the night? There are enough references to his practice of doing this to make it one of the most significant things that we can learn about his prayer life.

The gospel writers tell us that he went apart to pray before crucial decisions such as the calling of the disciples (Luke 6:12), and before major experiences like the transfiguration and the cross (Luke 9:28; Matt 26:36). He sought solitude when he knew there were going to be heavy demands on him for teaching and healing (Mark 1:35) and after important events such as the feeding of the five thousand (Matt 14:23; Mark 6:46). But his need for solitude was not always crisis-orientated, nor only to gather energy, assimilate experience, seek guidance or pour out requests – though doubtless all these aspects found their place in his prayer from time to time.

The still centre

He had a deep need to be alone, silent and still, *simply because he was human*. 'A life without a lonely place, that is, a life without a quiet center, easily becomes destructive'[1] and, we might add, shallow, dissipated and lacking in any sense of direction. We get nowhere if we fear to walk alone. The busier life is, the more need there is for a still centre; a place deep within us to which we can withdraw after the day-to-day buffeting and storms; a place where we can reflect on experience and try and make sense of life; a place where we can mull over events and savour them more fully; a place where, above all, we can listen . . . to what others are saying verbally or non-verbally, to what our feelings and fears are saying to us, and to what God is saying through circumstances, through people, through creation and his word spoken in the depths of our being. All these things pass us by, like views from the window of an express train, if we do not learn to stand still at disciplined intervals and do some stock-taking and viewing.

It was such a still centre that Jesus exhorted his disciples to cultivate, and surely they must have been impressed at the obvious and costly priority he gave to it himself. In Luke 6:12, we read that '*in these days* he went out to the mountain to pray'. The use of the plural here would suggest not a single, somewhat exceptional occasion but a regular part of his devotional pattern.

We have only to reflect upon the average day in the life of Jesus during his ministry to see why he regarded it as essential. In the normal course of the day he was never without human company. Even if our companions are self-chosen, as his disciples were, always to be surrounded by other people can be a great strain. Imagine what emotional and spiritual resources Jesus must have needed to hold together in relative harmony so heterogeneous a collection of men with such different backgrounds, education, practical skills, political persuasions and so on . . . and not large enough a group to dilute the tensions or avoid confrontation!

Then, too, there was the sensitive nurturing of this little group to bring them to the point where they would grasp who it really was who had called them to follow him, and what discipleship to *this* teacher would involve. There were many teachers in the days of Jesus, each with a group of disciples. None would have been preparing his little band for a final catastrophic event in the way that Jesus was. He had the delicate task of judging the right moment to awaken their perception to the truth about their relationship to him and their own future world-changing role. This kind of knowledge could not be forced prematurely. He needed time and space to reflect on how to handle it and to listen to the Father to know *his* mind.

Besides his disciples, Jesus was rarely without a crowd around him. His own personal space was constantly invaded – not just in terms of time but in actual physical contact. Jostled and pushed by the throng (Mark 5:31), forced to preach from a borrowed boat in order to distance himself a little from the growing crowd on the shore (Matt 13:2), the picture builds up of someone under incessant pressure. When those who brought their paralytic friend for healing 'could not get near him because of the crowd' (Mark 2:4), they removed the roof above him to lower the pallet at his feet. He had no body-guards or security men, and even when the disciples sought to protect him it didn't always help. His compassion for the crowds meant that mothers came crashing in with their children. No matter how tired he felt, he always seemed to have time for *them*. Did he perhaps find their candour and innocence refreshing in the face of so much devious adult behaviour?

This need for space was genuine, however, and Jesus had no compunction in catering for it, even when it appeared that he was spurning cries for help. There were times when he quite definitely turned away from people. 'Seeing the crowds' he escaped and 'went up on the mountain' (Matt 5:1) to be apart with his disciples for some quality time together. On another occasion, when his disciples tracked him down and said, 'Every one is searching for you' (Mark 1:37), his response was to go to another town. He refused to submit to the tyranny of the urgent. He would not let the crowds or even human need dictate the priorities. He had the inner freedom to say 'No.' In this particular gospel incident, it is directly *after* a prolonged period of solitude that Jesus is able to refuse, for in his silence he has discerned God's priorities and gained

God's perspectives. His energy, being human, is limited; but, in prayer, he understands more clearly how it is to be harnessed for the greater glory of God.

Not in bondage to the need to achieve, nor neurotic about the success of his mission, nor puffed up by popularity, he is free. He can weave his way safely through the continual manipulations of men. Simply because he has been alone, he is in touch with the wellsprings of his life; he has stood in the presence of his Father, becoming centred again, willing one will with him, absorbing the clean atmosphere of truth and developing the kind of clarity of vision which can pierce through falsity. That is why we need to heed his example of seeking the lonely place – to have that inner freedom and sure touch of discernment.

Unlike him, we may not often be able to get away to the hills or isolated spots (except perhaps on holiday). Geography and climate may rule out, for much of the year, that blissful solitude that we find out of doors in the beauties of nature. Small houses and urban environments may make it extremely difficult to get any actual *physical* solitude, silence or space. Yet, without question, they are important; as Mme Guyon said, 'External silence is most necessary to cultivate the internal; and indeed 'tis impossible to become inward without loving silence and retirement.'[2] Thomas Merton was even more emphatic: 'When you gain interior silence you can carry it around with you in the world, and pray everywhere. But just as interior asceticism cannot be acquired without concrete and exterior mortification, so it is absurd to talk about interior silence where there is no exterior silence.'[3]

If then, we are to cultivate the inner realities, we must seize and make opportunities for the external expressions. Maybe we can do it by planning a retreat or quiet day from time to time, or by sometimes choosing quite deliberately to take a solitary walk or drive, or by sitting quietly in a garden, park or church knowing we shall be undisturbed.

We need to learn, possibly painfully, the value of doing nothing. 'Sometimes I sits and thinks', said the old peasant, 'and sometimes I just sits.' Contemporary attitudes have instilled in us such guilt feelings about being unproductive, we drive ourselves in a perpetual frenzy of non-stop activity. And, let's face it, often tied up in all our good works and packed programmes is a need to justify ourselves. In whose eyes? Our own? Other people's? Or God's? Even though we know full well – in our hearts – that we do not need to, indeed cannot, justify ourselves in God's sight through works, we still behave as though we believe we can. We are justified by faith, and that faith needs the right environment in which to grow – the environment of silence and solitude.

When we can bring ourselves to stop and carve out time to be alone with God, we may find that our experience has something in common with that of Gerard Hughes when he spent a month in complete solitude on a small island off the west coast of Scotland. With no company but that of the island sheep, no access to telephone, post, TV, newspapers or radio, he was in total silence, except for the sound of wind, waves and the gulls overhead.

Sitting, watching, gazing became the pattern of my days. The beauty and peace of this lovely isle began to take hold of me. It was like an inner cleansing of the mind and senses. I began to notice simple things, the rocks, the stones, the shells, the wild flowers, the birds and gulls as though I were seeing them for the first time, and I never grew tired of looking. It was the same with spiritual truths. If I put into words the things I learned I write platitudes and clichés, but the island . . . taught me the value of platitudes.

Silence, I had always known, is helpful for prayer, and I used to try and keep silence in retreats, but keeping silence can be a noisy business and does not necessarily still the spirit. The island silence was of a different kind. *I did not 'practise' silence; it took hold of me.* Prayer became much less of an exercise and more of a repose. God is everywhere and God is mystery. I already knew that was true, but on the island there was the space and time to relish the truth, to be seized and permeated by it.[4]

This surely, must have been the experience of Jesus, too, as he went out to a lonely place?

> O Sabbath rest by Galilee!
>   O calm of hills above,
> Where Jesus knelt to share with thee
> The silence of eternity,
>   Interpreted by love![5]

Here, John Greenleaf Whittier captures very vividly the sense of peace on the hillside, the silence that was so rich, nourishing, creative . . . and moreish! We can picture Jesus revelling in the intense stillness, his awareness heightened by the sounds of silence. He withdrew to those places where his senses would be on tiptoe leading him to wonder. He chose spots where marvellous panoramic views and the sweep of the heavens could evoke awe, and where, too, he could find God in the 'little things' – the blade of grass, the lily, the sparrow, the lamb, the fox.

On those occasions, albeit rare ones, when we *can* get to the hills or the sea or forest or river, and enter into both outer and inner solitude, we too will share the silence of eternity. But we have to educate ourselves to it – it will not be altogether easy at first. We may feel distracted, uncomfortable or, once again, guilty. It requires a little perseverance to discover the joys to be found. As Rainer M. Rilke has said:

> He who for the first time has Thee in his keeping
> is disturbed by his neighbour and his watch;
> He walks bent over Thy footprints
> as if laden and burdened with years.
> Only later does he draw near to nature,
> Becomes aware of the winds and the far distances,
> hears Thy whisper in the meadows,
> worships Thee in song from the stars
> and can never again unlearn Thee,
> for everything is but Thy mantle.[6]

Some people are unnerved by too much silence. They feel it is not for them. At one school, pupils doing their A level exams asked for pop music to be played in the exam hall because they found the silence too disturbing. Other people seem to need the radio going all day – for company? To stave off the need to listen to what is happening inside? To shut out unwelcome demands?

Obviously, some people are temperamentally happier with silence than others; but, even so, we all need a certain degree of it for wholeness and sanity. We need never feel it is phoney or self-indulgent.

There are, however, such practical difficulties as noisy children, endless telephone calls, juggernauts hurtling by and jumbo jets roaring overhead. We live in a noise-polluted world and silence, actual physical silence, *can* often only be found in the heart of the country away from the flight paths. But real silence is not necessarily incompatible with outward noise and tensions. One of the Solitaries of our Community has her hermitage in the grounds of the Convent bordering an exceedingly busy and noisy thoroughfare. Yet she lives a life of deep interior silence.

Each of us needs an oasis now and again, but if we live and work for most of the year amidst noise, and noise is our inescapable desert, we can still receive Christ's gift of peace and carry it into that desert situation. Safeguarding the gift within, we can bring it into areas where it will disturb false peace. And isn't it true that our own noise and inner din can often be far more disruptive to real peace and silence than the juggernauts and the jumbo jets?

It was precisely because of these practical difficulties that Jesus told his disciples to cultivate a still centre *inside themselves*. 'When you pray, go into your room and shut the door and pray to your Father who is in secret' (Matt 6:6). Some of his hearers may have been fortunate enough to have a private room. The majority would not. The ordinary Palestinian home was 'open plan' and most people would have had even less privacy than the average Westerner today. Jesus must, therefore, have been speaking not only of a secret place as opposed to display in prayer but of that 'portable inner sanctuary'[7] which we carry around with us and to which we can withdraw at any time and in any place. Waiting for a bus, at the doctor's surgery, during a tea break, wherever or whatever, we are free to move back and forth across the threshold of this inner place of solitude and prayer, to commune with God unnoticed and unknown by any other human being. It is like a perpetual wayside shrine at which we can pause and worship throughout the day's work.

In the days of ancient augury, the colleges of priests who practised divination used to mark out a special enclosure in which to observe the flight of birds. From their observations they uttered their oracles. The enclosure was called a 'templum', and gradually the word 'templum' came to mean any enclosure especially marked out in order to step into it and encounter numinous and spiritual forces. It could be used of a sacred grove of trees, a magic circle, a ring of giant stones, and of course it came to be used of buildings erected for this purpose – 'temples'.[8]

In Psalm 132, David says: 'I will not come within the tabernacle of mine house: nor climb up into my bed; I will not suffer mine eyes to sleep, nor mine eye-lids to slumber . . . until I find out a place for the temple of the Lord' (Ps 132:3–5 Coverdale).

So zealous was he to create a worthy resting place for the ark of God, which for most of its history had been mobile, he could not sleep – not until he had marked out a place for the 'templum', or enclosure, which would provide permanent shelter and settlement for the divine presence in their midst. And he sees the longing as mutual. For God says: 'This shall be my rest for ever; here will I dwell for I have a delight therein' (v. 14).

The Jerusalem temple of David's dream and Solomon's fulfilment was a material one. But Jesus spoke of *himself* as a temple, and scandalised his critics by predicting that if it were destroyed, he would rebuild it in three days (John 2:19–21). St Paul tells us that our bodies are temples of the Holy Spirit (1 Cor 3:16; 6:19). We have become the living temples of a living God, and yet, paradoxically, we need to stake out the boundaries of that enclosure again and again, to mark out that 'templum' and inner enclosure for the Lord which is his and his alone, where he longs to 'make his rest for ever' and 'delights to dwell therein', but which can so easily become cluttered up or eroded. And we ourselves step into that enclosure to meet with spiritual forces, to encounter the Lord himself. But we only cultivate the habit of going in and out of the 'templum' throughout the day, if we have first established it in solitude and silence, and maintained its upkeep by regular and more prolonged periods within it. For the activity proper to the 'templum' is *contemplation*.

Even though we are free to mark out the inner space for God, it is nevertheless of immense help if we are able to have an *actual* material 'templum' too.

Most of us will never taste the utter solitude of a remote island as Gerard Hughes did. Escape to the hills, lakes or forest may be only very occasional. But though the setting may be different, the discovery can be the same – that silence can take hold of us.

Since by nature we are such scattered, fragmented creatures, we often need to be localised in prayer. It is helpful to mark out a 'templum' which, whenever we come to it, will have for us immediate associations of prayer. It will reduce the time it takes to settle and centre down[9] (unfamiliar places often have their distractions) and will enable us to slip quickly into silence and inner communion with the Lord.

Of Aiden W. Tozer it is written that 'a dingy corner of the basement of the family home became his private prayer chamber'.[10] There are more contemporary examples which might give *us* practical ideas. A built-in wardrobe was converted into a prayer-room by one, a cleaned-up coal cellar became an oratory for another. But even that amount of space may be impossible in many modern homes. A particular chair, table or desk can equally be a praying place, or just a corner of the bedroom, with perhaps a visual focus. Once we have established our 'templum', however simple, it disposes of the question 'Where?' We are still left, however, with the other questions of 'When?' and 'How?'

It will never be easy. Time will always be at a premium, but it really is a top priority, not an optional extra, in Christian discipleship. Jesus made that very clear by precept and example. Safeguarding time in the inner sanctuary will cut out a lot of wastage and fruitless endeavour. It will ensure that we operate from a God-centre and not that self-centre where we are controlled by all manner of subtle forms of self-seeking and ambition. The Holy Spirit is perfectly able to untangle our very mixed motives if we give him the opportunity, and stop running away from the painful truths that he may expose in our solitude.

> In solitude we can slowly unmask the illusion of our possessiveness and discover in the center of our own self that we are not what we can conquer, but what is given to us . . . that being is more important than having, and that we are worth more than the result of our efforts . . . that our worth is not the same as our usefulness.[11]

The desert

It was not always to the gentle hills of Galilee that Jesus went to be alone. As we have seen, he frequented the desert as a praying place, too – that unfriendly, frightening place that has nevertheless drawn man to it all down through the ages, teased his imagination and called him tantalisingly to explore it. In 1974, Geoffrey Moorhouse published *The Fearful Void*. Interviewing him on TV, Jonathan Dimbleby asked 'What is it about the desert that obsesses Western man? Why is it a *mysterium tremendens et fascinans*? What creates this love–hate relationship with the most desolate areas on the face of the earth?'

Surely it is partly the vastness, the great silence, the fact that the desert draws forth from man a heroic quality of endurance. It is the place where to be lost is terrifying. The desert somehow puts man in perspective, reminds him of his insignificance and littleness. In its vast trackless wastes he becomes a vulnerable, infinitesimal dot on the landscape. That, of course, constitutes an enormous challenge – and always will. Even if man has come to terms with the desert, he has not overcome it.

The desert is also one of the Bible's most powerful images. It is the place of retreat and withdrawal, not flight from reality but the entrance into a profounder reality; the place of terror and trial; the place where you come to God and you come to yourself; the place of vision and prophetic insight; the place where you discover your identity and vocation, where the spiritual struggle is most intense and the awareness of angels and demons most acute.

No lambs and lilies here, but scorpions, vipers, rats and thorns. No soft breezes and lapping waves, but intense heat by day, bitter cold by night and the howling wind sweeping across the empty spaces like the eerie cries of many demons.

This was the place to which Jesus withdrew for at least one lengthy period of prayer and fasting, when the Spirit compelled him to go into the wilderness following his baptism (Mark 1:12). The moment of vision gave way to intense struggle. During that time (and there may well have been others) he faced all the horror of self-questioning and self-doubt, the temptation to enter the power game and ensure success for his mission, to attract attention and win converts through sensational methods, to take the enticing path of compromise which would provide an escape clause to suffering. There, in solitude, he wrestled with the world's standards and shunned them for those of the kingdom.

Let us never fool ourselves that the desert offers an escape from the world, the flesh and the devil. The desert fathers and their successors in hermitages all over the world have not chosen a soft option. They engage in spiritual warfare in a particularly concentrated way. All of us are called to it some of the time. They, on their frontier posts, are called to it most of the time.

Jesus withdrew to the Judean desert. His successors in this kind of solitude have lived in the Sahara, Sinai, Patmos,

Mount Athos, Petra, Iona, Tamanrasset, Glasshampton, Norwich, Kentucky, up-state New York, Manchester, Cerne Abbas, Bardsey Island, Wantage . . . a whole host of places where hermits have gone in the footsteps of Jesus, 'out to a very lonely place' commissioned by the church to wage their spiritual warfare in solitude, but also in solidarity with all mankind.

For us the desert may not be the Sahara but the inner city, the hospital bed, the concrete jungle, the kitchen or the Senior Common Room. The environment may vary. The challenge does not.

Spiritual warfare

It was to meet this very challenge that Jesus went out into the desert. Spiritual warfare is a courageous work of prayer which calls us not only to search our own hearts but to plunge deeply into the heart of the world of which we continue to be a part even when we feel we have withdrawn from it, albeit temporarily. Solitude is not the same thing as separation. This touches on Charles Williams' concept of the 'co-inherence' of mankind.

We withdraw from the world not only to search our own heart but in order to plunge deep into the heart of the world, and 'to listen more intently to the deepest and most neglected voices that proceed from its inner depths'.[12]

Withdrawal into solitude has much in common with underwater swimming. We know that sounds carry over great distances in the depths – hence the extraordinary transatlantic conversations of whales which can be heard as they sing and moan to each other across the miles.

Similarly, in prayer, we can plunge into a deep silence and 'pick up' the inarticulate cries of human suffering. In the depths of prayer we may, for example, be tuned in to the silent voices of the prisoners of conscience or the silent world of autism, and share the pain of both. This kind of listening was surely part of Jesus' prayer.

There is even more to this underwater swimming, however.

Other things lurk in the watery deeps beside sound waves. It is worth remembering that 'the deep' to the Jew was the place of chaos and danger. Leviathan, whom God 'formed to sport in the deep' lived there along with many other menacing creatures. Chaos is that part of creation as yet unredeemed. So it was a place of hidden terror, a place where one battled for existence, where to be swallowed up meant separation from God and man.

Spiritual warfare is no less fearsome, for it is there, in the depths, that the enemy lurks. But we are called to plunge in, 'to penetrate those primeval depths where man's need is at its greatest and the forces of disintegration are at work.'[13]

In his novel *The Cruel Sea*, Nicholas Monsarrat tells of the agonising decision that a captain had to make when one of the destroyers in his convoy was torpedoed. As the stricken ship went down, the heads of survivors could be seen bobbing about in the water like so much human flotsam and jetsam. He ordered his own ship to go full steam ahead for a rescue operation, but as he did so, the radar operator picked up the signals of an enemy submarine lying immediately beneath the men. The choice, for the captain, lay between an attempt to rescue the survivors with the almost certain destruction of another ship and many more lives, or going for the hidden enemy in the depths and destroying the submarine! Salvation or destruction was his choice. And yet it was no choice. In the circumstances he could not be saviour to those men, for he had to go to the root of the evil and do battle there. Consequently the survivors were blown up with the submarine and the captain lived with the lifelong torment of what he had been forced to do.

It illustrates the problem we may well face if we engage in spiritual warfare. In order to go to the depths and do battle with the enemy who lurks there, we shall sometimes have to ignore the cries of distress on the surface.

It is not easy to stand by in an apparent impotence, but we have to turn away resolutely from any Messiah-complex which tries to do everything and in the end achieves very little. It is not lack of compassion that forces us to do this. On the contrary, 'it is in solitude that . . . compassionate solidarity takes its shape'.[14]

When we have to turn from the surface cries and clamour for a greater need, we are simply following in the footsteps of Jesus who himself chose the solitude of the desert to do battle not with a particular manifestation of evil but with the very root of evil itself.

Discovering who we are

Everywhere we see people wrapped in the isolation that comes from a constant bombardment of noise. It stops us communicating with each other. A young man admitted to me that, when travelling, he wore his Sony Walkman earphones in order to stop others trying to converse with him. All this noise creates loneliness rather than solitude, and division rather than unity within ourselves.

The Quakers used to speak of a silence that 'sifts' us, and it sifts out the things inside us that we are not always happy to discover.

'When one enters the desert (whether real or metaphorical) without books and magazines, without radio and TV, when one's senses are no longer bombarded by all the junk to which we are ordinarily exposed, when the top layers of our psyche are swept clean and bare and empty – then the deeper layers of the 'psyche' rise to the surface. The inner demons lift up their ugly faces.'[15]

But what is the alternative? To ignore them and leave them buried, sapping us of vital energy and preventing growth? Are we to go on in illusion and pretence – all the while sitting on a time bomb? For, sooner or later, the inner demons will do more than lift their ugly faces. They will erupt, get out of control, break free like a lion from its cage, and destroy.

We all have within us an extraordinary mixture of beautiful and ugly, strong and weak, light and shadow. We prefer not to know about the negative side of our personality, but solitude gives us the chance to get in touch with our own chaos, to own

it and allow it to be redeemed. As James Thurber put it:
'Inside every Little Nell there is a Lady Macbeth trying to
get out.'[16] She needs redemption. Jesus said, 'Love your
enemies.' 'But what if I should discover that the very enemy
himself is within me, that I myself am the enemy who must
be loved – WHAT THEN?'[17] It is the story of Beauty
and the Beast. 'We must learn to kiss the Beast in ourselves . . . because that is God's work of total acceptance in
us.'[18]

Letting go of our illusions and masks is a frightening
business – and a costly one. In calling his book about deserts
The Fearful Void, Geoffrey Moorhouse was not simply
referring to the Sahara. Part of the challenge which lay behind
his exploit was to come to terms with the fearful void that he
suspected lay at the centre of his being. It is the dread of
us all. As we make this journey inward and the masks are
stripped away, we *do* begin to fear that we shall ultimately
come to nothing. What if I should arrive at an empty
core, a no-being, what Kierkegaard called 'the existential
dread'?

Jesus gives us the clue. He was Son of God. At baptism his
sonship was affirmed. Immediately after, in the long testing
period of the desert, that inner knowledge was challenged
repeatedly, '*If* you are the Son of God, then . . .' He, too, had
to face the insidious doubts that were thrown across the path
of his growing self-awareness. But solitude is the crucible of
transformation, and during the forty days in the wilderness
his sense of identity grew in strength and certainty. Denis
Potter's controversial film, *Son of Man*, depicted a Christ, in
the fearful emptiness of the wilderness, almost writhing in
spiritual and mental agony and crying 'Am I? Am I the Son of
God?'

An Oxford don who journeyed through a desert, as part of
an inner pilgrimage, told me that three days into the desert
she was hallucinating, so extraordinarily powerful is the effect
of that vast space and nothingness.

Is it irreverent to wonder whether or not Jesus had to
struggle with the fear that he was suffering from the strange

effects that the desert, loneliness and hunger can have on the mind? Even if that is not so, we can be sure that it was a time of fierce and terrible struggle, and the answers to the doubts, self-questioning and subtle suggestions of the Evil One did not drop from his lips without effort or pain.

Having gone through that test, however, his own sense of sonship was tempered like steel.

We, too, are 'sons of God', our identity is assured in baptism. God confirms us in the truth of our relationship with him. It is unlikely that any of us escapes some attack on that experiential knowledge. We have our moments of deep certainty, but there are also for us the times of insidious and shattering doubt when we begin to wonder, 'Am I? Am I really a child of God? Or do I entertain illusions of grandeur? *If* I were a child of God, then . . . I wouldn't be like this, or he wouldn't allow the other, etc.' We can push these questions aside in our busyness, but they won't just go away. They lurk around to pop up again when we are feeling particularly weak, or in the face of a crisis. At such times of testing, perhaps the last thing we *want* is solitude. We'd rather keep the pain at bay by immersing ourselves in more activity. Yet, it is actually in solitude and silence, as we spread our doubts before the Lord, without any attempt to wrap them up nicely or pretend they are other than what they are, that we receive confirmation of our relationship with the Father, that our sense of identity as his child goes through a tempering process and we discover more of our true being. P. T. Forsyth realised this when he said that, in prayer we get rid of illusions about ourselves and the world because true prayer is encounter with the living God who is reality. 'Those who cannot be alone cannot find their true being and they are always something less than themselves.'[19]

The fruit of solitude

So then, solitude leads to a deepening relationship with God and others, an encounter with evil and a discovery or confirmation of identity. It is a journey into oneself, yet not selfish. No mere ego trip, this. No self-indulgent devotional exercise.

We may be *driven* into the 'desert' by the expulsive power of the Holy Spirit, as Jesus was, because it expands our capacity for feeling, it strengthens our appeal against falsity. It becomes part of our prayer for the world as we gain new perspectives by distancing ourselves from it for a while. For the desert has its own horizons.

'Unless a man takes himself *out* of the world by retirement and self-reflection, he will be in danger of losing himself *in* the world,' said Dr Benjamin Whichcote, Provost of King's College, Cambridge in the seventeenth century.[20]

Before me, as I write, is the photograph of an original icon painted by Dr Militza Zernov of Oxford. It depicts 'Jesus Christ the Perfect Silence'. On the face of the youthful figure of Christ pain and sorrow mingle with a kind of questioning expression.

In iconography, silence is usually signified by a finger touching the lips. Here, however, it is symbolised by folded hands. This is the silence of non-action, rest, patience, long-suffering, goodness, meekness. It is the Christ who stands back and weeps over the city because it does not know the things that belong to its peace. It represents the true silence of patience and suffering – supremely the silence of the passion.

It is 'the stature of waiting'.[21] 'He does not judge the world but leaves it free.'[22]

It speaks of the mystery of a God who suffers the havoc man has created, and of a silence that heals and saves. And it is the fruit of solitude.

We are back, then, to where we started this chapter. Jesus needed solitude simply because he was human – the only fully human person who has ever lived. He sought solitude as 'an active resistance to all that would dehumanise men by reducing them to unreflecting functionaries'. He believed that 'the internal freedom which true solitude discloses is the heritage of every person and constitutes the human dignity of each'.[23]

Lovelonging for God

For all these reasons, it would seem that Jesus went out to a lonely place to pray. But they are still not the foremost reason. Nor should they be ours.

He went apart to cure his loneliness. He needed the silence of eternity as a thirsting man in the desert needs water. And he essentially needed the silence of eternity which was *interpreted by love*. For he who was love incarnate had his own needs to love and be loved. His deepest need, and likewise ours, could be met only by God. Ultimately no human being, no matter how close or dear, can fully satisfy our need for love. Those who imagine they can end up devouring one another.

Jesus longed for time apart to bask and sunbathe in his Father's love, to soak in it and repose in it. No matter how drained he felt, it seems that this deep, silent communion refreshed him more than a good night's sleep.

'The Lover longed for solitude, and went away to be alone, that he might gain the companionship of his Beloved, for amid many people he was lonely.'[24]

Just to be alone with his Father, that was his deepest longing. This converted his loneliness into solitude. It is the easiest thing in the world to react to loneliness by searching for a way out which uses someone or something to fill the aching void. Human love and friendship indeed enrich our lives and partly meet this need – but not entirely, for at the core of our being a 'transcendental neediness holds sway',[25] a lovelonging for God which will only be met by converting our loneliness into deep solitude, by fleeing the sweets and cordials that may give temporary satisfaction, and finding the real thing in *him*.

The psalmists knew this. Here are some verses from Psalm 42 (NTW) which bear this out:

> As the deer pants after the water brooks:
> so longs my soul for you, O God.
> My soul is thirsty for God, thirsty for the living God:
> when shall I come and see his face?

These are all attempts to express the inexpressible, that hunger and thirst after God that is beautitude, and which one day will be wholly satisfied when after sifting and purification our capacity is enlarged to receive him.

And in that Love which is wayless, we shall wander and stray, and it shall lead us and lose us in the immeasurable breadth of the love of God. And herein we shall flee forth and flee out of ourselves, into the unknown raptures of the goodness and riches of God. And therein we shall melt and be melted away, and shall eternally wander and sojourn within the glory of God.[26]

(See the Appendix for practical follow-up suggestions.)

3

'ABBA' – intimate prayer

He was praying in a certain place, and when he ceased, one
of his disciples said to him, 'Lord, teach us to pray, as John
taught his disciples.' And he said to them, 'When you pray,
say: "Father, hallowed be thy name . . ."'

(Luke 11:1,2)

The disciples' question

All night in prayer, frequently wandering off to the 'certain
places' of which the gospel writers speak (Luke 11:1) for long
periods of solitude – what kind of prayer was this? What was
the secret of the serenity, the inner strength and the authority
which seemed to flow from Jesus when he returned from these
prayer sessions? Did the disciples feel awed, slightly uncomfortable or even envious? Or did they perhaps feel all these
things at once? There must have been something – a quality,
an atmosphere – which they realised was different from
anything they had met before, in themselves or others.

How, they might have wondered, did he actually spend the
time? They knew he would be familiar with the liturgical
prayers of their people. Perhaps these found some place in the
nights of prayer? Devout Jews used to love to meditate upon
the law and recite the psalms. They, too, might have been
included. Was intercession also one aspect of this secret
prayer life?

Whatever their speculations and questions, something
about the Lord's pattern of prayer led them to ask for

teaching. They would be aware, and perhaps impressed, that John the Baptist had given his disciples specific instruction. It was customary for a rabbi to train his disciples in a particular prayer which became a distinguishing mark of that group. So it was a perfectly natural expectation that Jesus' disciples expressed when they asked him to teach them to pray.

It could, however, have been far more than the fulfilment of a custom that prompted them. Perhaps the immediate reason was the example of Jesus himself. 'A prayerful life, with a character to match, is a better invitation to prayer than many exhortations.'[1]

That truth still applies. The saint who has 'penetrated the veil and has gazed with the inward eye upon the wonder that God is'[2] will inspire far more people to pray than any number of books on the subject. True holiness is always attractive.

Jesus' novel emphasis – a personal relationship

What a pity it is that we can't see the stunned looks on the faces of the disciples as Jesus immediately acceded to their request – for stunned they must surely have been by his first words. 'When you pray,' said Jesus, 'say: Father . . .'

Now the idea of the fatherhood of God was not new. The Old Testament has a number of references to it. For example in the Psalms:

> As a father is tender towards his children:
> so is the Lord tender to those that fear him
> Ps 103:13 (NTW)

Or Isaiah: 'thou, O Lord, art our Father, our Redeemer from of old is thy name' (Isa 63:16). In Malachi 2:10 we read, 'Have we not all one father? Has not one God created us?' And in Isaiah 64:8, 'thou art our Father; we are the clay, and thou art our potter'.

Apart from the specific references, there are also beautiful word pictures, such as the one in Hosea where Israel is described as a son, 'When Israel was a child, I loved him, and out of Egypt I called my son' (Hos 11:1). Later in the same chapter (Hos 11:3,4) he describes himself as a father taking them up in his arms, putting them on leading reins and teaching them to walk, bending down to feed them.

Nor are we given only father pictures. Isaiah speaks of God as Mother: 'As one whom his mother comforts, so I will comfort you' (Isa 66:13).

It was not then the *idea* of God as Father that was startling. It was the invitation to address him as such that was entirely new. Whatever other question marks may be held over the recorded sayings of Jesus regarding their authenticity, of this we can be confident. These words really are his. There is no doubt, whatsoever, that Jesus taught his disciples to pray, 'Father'.

Not only so, we have the unanimous testimony of the four gospels that at all times he did so himself. He set the pattern that was to continue on into the life and prayer of the church (Rom 8:15; Gal 4:6). And notice, he didn't use the determinative form (i.e. the father), 'rather it is a vocative form, 'Father', originally a piece of childish chatter'.[3]

Professor Joachim Jeremias tells us that 'The result of a search for Jewish parallels to the use of *abba* as a form of address in prayers proves completely negative[4] . . . *There is not a single example of the use of* abba . . . *as an address to God in the whole of Jewish literature.*'[5]

To the Jew, 'Abba' is a very familiar form of address. *Abba* and *Imma* were the first words a child learnt to say, and even though, by the time of Jesus, the use was no longer restricted simply to very young children, yet it was a very personal and familiar term by which no one had ever before dared to address God.

That was what was so exceptional about it. That is why the disciples might have looked stupefied. For Jesus was introducing an entirely new way of approaching God. To men who had previously been reluctant even to utter the name of God — a God who, for all his fatherly love, was a somewhat remote figure 'high and lifted up', governing the nations, ruling the waves, creating and re-creating, King over all the earth, meting out judgment and mercy, and separated by his awful holiness – suddenly to call him 'Daddy' was unthinkable! Even Moses, who spoke to God face to face as a friend, didn't go that far. We are not told how the disciples reacted to this extraordinary exhortation, but we can imagine they might well have been appalled.

Yet, in introducing it, Jesus was teaching them that prayer is more than offering praise and worship, confession and petition. It is the expression of an intimate relationship with God.

Old Testament writers could speak of 'loving the law' (Ps 119) and 'loving wisdom' (Prov 29:3), but they were manifestations of God rather than God himself. To immerse oneself within them was to be immersed in God – but there was always that one-degree-removed aspect of them. So holy was the Lord God, he could not be approached or touched directly (Exod 33:20). He had need of types and shadows.

There is of course the nuptial imagery of Hosea and the Song of Solomon, where Israel takes on the role of bride. But brides of the eighth century BC had a very different standing in Judaism from our twentieth century AD Western custom. She was the property of her husband, bound to him by a covenant which was not necessarily one of equality and intimacy.

Daily a Jew would recite the *Shema* – 'Hear, O Israel: The Lord our God is one Lord; and you shall love the Lord your God with all your heart, and with all your soul, and with all your might' (Deut 6:4,5). Love was commanded from man. Love was freely given by God as part of the covenant relationship. The steadfast love of the Lord would stand for ever, his mercies would endure. Great tenderness is implied, but nothing to equal the intimacy and homeliness of 'Abba'.

God was personal – of that the Jew was in no doubt. But he did not necessarily *experience* him as personal, i.e. have a personal relationship with him. In any case, his relationship would be as a member of the Jewish nation, not as an individual.

'Personality and fatherhood carry with them the idea of the

possibility of intimate acquaintance' and A. W. Tozer main-
tains that, as for the Jew, so for millions of Christians, the
possibility of personal acquaintance is no more real than to a
non-Christian: 'They go through life trying to love an ideal
and be loyal to a mere principle.'[6]

The first thing, then, that Jesus taught his disciples about
prayer was that it involved relationship. In doing so, he
opened a window for them on to the secret of his own prayer
life. The solitude and silence which he needed so much (why
else would he have sought them so regularly?) were spent rapt
in intimate communion with the God whom he loved personally and addressed as, 'Father'. This joy of intimacy is now
extended to the disciples and later, among early Christians,
would be the supreme privilege given to converts immediately
after baptism when they would be taught the Lord's Prayer. It
is true, is it not, that in everyday life the form of address we
use is a clue as to where we stand in our relationship with
someone? Stage one is to be introduced by name and title,
e.g. 'Mr Jones'. Stage two may be to omit the 'Mr' and just
'Jones' indicates a more familiar and equal status. When,
however, the formalities are dropped and Christian or first
names are invited, the relationship has clearly developed into
something far more friendly. An even deeper, more familiar,
stage of friendship has been reached when nicknames or
diminutives are used.

There are pet names within a family circle which no one
outside the family would presume, or be invited, to use.
'Abba' is a family title. It is as though Jesus is saying to his
friends, 'Come into the closer circle of the family. Let us
adopt you as a member of it. You are free to take advantage of
some of its privileges.' To use the title 'Father' is a sign not
simply of being part of the family but of being *children* within
it. It conjures up the picture of children running freely round
their home, scrambling on to their father's lap to share with
him all their concerns.

Where and when, we might wonder, did Jesus first adopt
this extraordinarily daring way of praying? Did he have a
deep sense even as a child of that oneness with the Father

which he claimed as an adult? Did he, even in those early years, find himself running freely and naturally to his Father in spirit, instinctively calling him 'Abba'? If so, one wonders what he called Joseph?

Or was it because in Joseph he saw all that was best in fatherhood that it was the most natural thing in the world to transfer the title to God?

We can't know. What is certain is that the only recorded words of Jesus in the first thirty years of his life have to do with a conflict of loyalties between Abba Joseph (and Mary) and Abba-Father (God).

'Did you not know that I must be in my Father's house?' (Luke 2:49). By the age of twelve, then, he was addressing God in this intimate way – and surely it reflects the growing sense of his special relationship with him. Mary, who had pondered many things in her heart from his birth upwards, would not have missed the implications of this 'Abba'. It would be a sign to her that her son was growing in wisdom and inner knowledge as well as in stature.

Now, however, he wants his disciples to share this sense of intimate relationship, to come into the experience which St Paul spoke of later, when he said that in the kingdom we are not slaves but sons – sons by adoption and grace. Therefore we have been given the right to call God, 'Abba-Father', through the work of the Holy Spirit in us (Rom 8:15, 16).

Dependence

In teaching his disciples to begin their prayer in this way, Jesus was perhaps reinforcing his other injunction to 'become as little children'. By consenting to be children in the eyes of the heavenly Father, they would be acknowledging their dependence on him totally – in small things as well as large. Small children haven't yet been asked to take responsibility for themselves, so they know how to be dependent in humble, simple, childlike trust – unless for some reason that trust has been smashed by a father who has given them counterfeit gifts . . . stones instead of bread, an eel instead of a fish, a sleeping scorpion curled up to look like an egg.

It is the defenceless (babies, very young animals, the elderly, the handicapped) who often display a moving quality of simple trust which, in turn, draws out great gentleness on the part of others. Somehow it is so much easier to love and respond to that defencelessness than to the self-assured competence of others. God, too, finds the admission of weakness more lovable because it is nearer the truth. One of the most endearing things about the mentally handicapped is their simplicity. They are what they are. Reality shines out of them. No wonder the Orthodox Church calls them 'the holy ones'! However confident we may *seem*, without a right dependence on God we are extremely insecure. He longs for us to find him as our security and to stop trying to be our own gods, independent, capable and self-reliant. When we acknowledge our status as his *children* then he can act on our behalf for, remember 'he only likes youngsters in his kingdom'! It is as 'youngsters' that we experience his tender, protective love. It is as 'youngsters' that we have the freedom to drop our anxieties and cares and let him handle them for us and are able to enjoy a trustful repose in his presence.

We are invited to express our childlike dependence on the Father in very practical, ordinary ways and to let him into every area of our lives, no matter how domestic or seemingly trivial. But it is a call to be childlike, not infantile. There is no suggestion that we should anaesthetise our intelligence. The man who prayed for guidance each morning as to which tie he should wear was being silly and praying unworthily. God has given the gift of reason and he expects us to use it.

Sometimes people feel they cannot pray in an emergency because it would be dishonest. Simply to turn to God for help when they feel desperate seems to be using him. There is truth in that. We can only respect the integrity of their reluctance. He is not a conjuror to wave the magic wand at occasional moments of crisis. Yet sometimes it is the sudden discovery that we can't cope that brings us to realise our need of God –

and he rejoices however we make that discovery if it leads us into relationship with him.

Nevertheless, dependence is an overall attitude – the element in which our entire life should be lived – not just a support system when we find we can no longer help ourselves. Dependence is not a matter of adapting God to our own needs and concerns but a reaching out to him on his terms.

Love

There is another aspect to the freedom of the children of God. 'A child with strong trust in its parents is encouraged by that very trust to ask all kinds of questions.'[7] The disciple who can address God as 'Abba' need not fear to use his critical faculties. He can question and reflect and reason without disrespect – as Jesus himself did. It will not diminish the trust or jeopardise the bond. It might do that in a human relationship where the parent is insecure, but with God it leads to maturity. It places us in a position to hear his secrets which he can neither share with the self-sufficient and overconfident nor with the hardened sceptic who is incapable of responding to holy mysteries. Have you noticed that it is children who often have uncanny perception, an ability to penetrate beyond the 'masks', to see visions (and they are *not* just overimaginative, susceptible children, any more than Samuel was)?

As children we all long for love – all need love, desperately. The fortunate ones don't even have to think about it. Loved and adored from the moment they are born, they bask securely in the glow of this parental love, accepting it as their birthright without question. Other children cannot be sure. Parents are not always good at expressing their love, even though it may be deep. For other children there is no certainty about the loving because it is inconsistent. It fluctuates with the moods and fortunes of their parents, dependent, so it seems, on outward circumstances. For such parents love does not provide the bedrock of their relationship with their children. For these children there is a constant, unspoken fear – fear that something could sever the bond entirely. They grow up with a need to manipulate situations to ensure that such a thing never happens. They do everything to impress their parents, and to earn love by winning approval – anything, rather than be rejected!

As children of God, however, we have *absolute* certainty. One of the Old Testament's favourite words to describe his covenant love with his people is 'steadfast': 'I trust in the steadfast love of God for ever and ever' (Ps 52:8); 'thou, O God, art my fortress, the God who shows me steadfast love' (Ps 59:17).

There is a rocklike dependability about God's love for us which does not rest on approval. Nor do we have to earn it by our successes. Sometimes we are disillusioned by the fallibility of human love. To a greater or lesser degree we all let each other down. With God, however, our dependence is fully justified and never disappointed, for he is not arbitrary in his loving.

That is not to say that there aren't times when we wonder how, if he loves us, certain things can befall us. And we may cry out. We have plenty of precedents for this kind of dismay in the Old Testament. But Jesus has shown us the Father who is wise and anxious to give only *good* gifts to his children and whom we are to run to in prayer crying, 'Abba (Daddy), why is this happening to me?' It is what Jesus himself did in the garden of Gethsemane. It is still Abba he speaks to as he prays: 'Father, if thou art willing, remove this cup from me; nevertheless not my will, but thine, be done' (Luke 22:42).

With the deep bonds of love between a father and child goes a longing to share, on the part of the father, and a longing to imitate, on the part of the child. My father was a priest, and when my younger brother was very small he wanted to be with 'Daddy' the whole time, doing whatever Daddy did. He trundled his diminutive wheelbarrow alongside his father's as they gardened together, and he watered flowers with a tiny watering can. More than simply *being* with his father, he wanted to copy him and be like him, mowing the lawn in a clerical collar far too large for him. Draped in a white sheet, he would conduct services for his long-suffering friends, and since 'Daddy' seemed to give people food and drink at the end of a service, the friends received digestive biscuits and water as they meekly knelt in a row.

Coveting time with the Father and becoming like him was what Paul wanted, 'That I might know him . . . and be conformed to his likeness.' Knowing and being known is the essence of love. To be known and loved utterly takes away all fear, for there is nothing left for the loved one to find out that might disillusion him or lessen his love.

As we pray saying, 'Father . . .', we invite that intimate knowledge, and express a desire to know 'even as also we are known' (cf. 1 Cor 13:12). Therein lies security.

Attitudes to be avoided

Jesus, in his unique sonship with the Father, used an intimate address, but he did not presume. Being on intimate terms does not mean being on *equal* terms. Even he did not 'snatch at equality with God' (Phil 2:6 NEB). God is always Father with a father's authority that requires submission. The prayer Jesus taught began startlingly enough with 'Abba', but continued 'Hallowed be thy name'. Intimacy is balanced with respect, familiar address by reverence, immanence by transcendence. This is no invitation to speak to God in a presumptuous manner. Particularly in public worship there is a need for dignity and reverence even if our prayer is extempore.

'Hallowed be thy name' gives us a sense of the majesty and holiness of God – 'the antiseptic element' that saves our prayer 'from lapsing into an easy-going sentimentalism'.[8]

The paradox of the close proximity and infinite distance of God should always stop us making things 'too snug and confiding'.[9] No one has expressed this need for balance more beautifully than Mother Julian of Norwich:

For it is the will of our courteous Lord that we should be as much at home with him as heart may think or soul desire. But we must be careful not to accept this privilege so casually that we forget our own courtesy. For our Lord himself is supremely friendly, and he is as courteous as he is friendly: he is very courteous.[10]

Nor is the invitation to pray 'Abba' an excuse for unhealthy individualism. It is not '*My* Father' but 'Our Father'. We belong to a large family. None of us is an 'only child'. 'Abba' implies belonging to a body, and we unite with the other members of that body in prayer to our one Father. Here the Eastern Orthodox Church has retained a balance that is often upset in the West. The West overemphasises the individual at the expense of the corporate. Whereas 'an Eastern Christian does not approach God as an isolated individual; he worships him as a member of the Body of Christ. His supplications do not rise up like the voice of a solo singer, they form part of a great choir in which all the Saints and all the sinners have their share.'[11]

The second Adam's achievement

When Jesus gave the gift of 'Abba' to his disciples he – the second Adam – restored to mankind something that the first Adam had lost. The concept of man's *original* intimacy with God was sometimes rendered by the church fathers in the Greek word *parrhesia* – free speech.[12] It describes the utter freedom of communication that Adam enjoyed with God. Before the fall he was able to converse familiarly with the God who came down to walk with him in the garden in the evenings. Adam was at one with himself, with the creatures around him and with God. The 'free speech' of which the fathers speak was a symbolic expression of the perfect adaptation to reality which came from the fact that man was what God intended him to be – himself. He had no guile or deception until the fall, no masks or illusions, no posing or posturing. He had intimate spiritual communication with his creator, because he was innocent.

At the fall, when through disobedience he sought not to be himself but 'as God', he deliberately settled for unreality and a lie about himself and his relationship with God. And thereafter he could not face God without a disguise.

Children share something of the primal innocence that Adam originally knew. In exhorting us to 'become as little children', Jesus yearned to restore to us our lost intimacy with God, to give us back the possibility of *parrhesia*.

This was the redemptive work of the second Adam. The writer of the letter to the Hebrews tells us that God pierces the gloom of unreality and cuts through the outer disguises by his word which is sharper than a two-edged sword dividing between truth and falsity, exposing the secrets of the heart. There is no creature that is not manifest in his sight – no hiding from God in the garden now, 'all are open and laid bare to the eyes of him with whom we have to do' (Heb 4:12,13). No masks, no disguises, no fig leaves!

However, the way that was blocked through disobedience is now opened up as a new and living way by the high priest who has passed into the heavens, Jesus the Son of God.

'Let us then with *parrhesia* – boldness, confidence, free speech, perfect communication – draw near to the throne of grace' (Heb 4:16).

There it is! The familiar converse, the primal intimacy lost by the first Adam is now restored to us by the second.

Painful healing

How do we know and experience that intimacy? Simply by trying – and by trying it simply. By accepting Christ's offer of this intimate address and breathing, 'Father' – allowing all the sense of security, tenderness, care, provision and love to flow over us. By allowing our memories to help us in prayer as we recall the good moments in our childhood and in our relationships with our fathers. By translating some of those feelings into our relationship with God and then allowing him to build on them so much more – beyond all that our understanding could conceive of fatherly love. Feelings, imagination, memory and reason, joined with reflection on scriptural passages, can combine to give us insight into God's love for his children and an experiential knowledge of him as Father.

What, however, if the image of 'Father' is a totally unhelpful one? What if every memory of 'Father' is disturbing and painful? Sadly, there are many who have not experienced a good relationship with their fathers – quite the reverse in fact. 'Father' conjures up for them pictures of brutality, violence, cruelty, drunkenness, marital infidelity, weakness and, perhaps, incest. Others for one reason or another cannot recall their fathers at all. We can sympathise with all those who might well want to reject Christ's invitation to address God as Father.

Perhaps for them the image of God the Mother is a help. Matthew pictures the God who protects and nurtures like a hen with her chicks (Mt 23:37). Human parents might forget their children, and neglect them, but not God.

For Julian of Norwich, God as Mother was a recurring theme: 'Thus Jesus Christ that doeth good against evil is our very Mother: we have our Being of Him – where the ground of Motherhood beginneth – with all the sweet Keeping of Love that endlessly followeth. As verily as God is our Father, so verily God is our Mother.'[13]

This, too, may not help the situation. Someone bereaved of both parents at an early age or at risk from his/her parents and taken into care might well prefer to get away from family images altogether. That is understandable.

It is hard to escape the fact, though, that so much of Jesus' teaching about God centres around his fatherhood.

Despite the painful memories, however, the teaching of Jesus *can* be related to our wounds. It is true that many of his stories were about fathers, but we can take the qualities of character which he pinpoints in these stories and look for ways in which we have seen them incarnated in *someone*, whether it be a relative, parent substitute, teacher or friend –

the person who cared enough to keep on coming after us when we tried to break off a relationship; the person who gave us our freedom despite knowing that we would make a mess of it; the person who was there waiting to receive us back, to pick up the pieces of our broken lives when we came crawling home; the patient, tolerant, suffering, upbuilding, generous love of someone who helped us to believe in ourselves and face the world with self-respect. It may have been a relationship which could not continue – but we learn wisdom even by loving unwisely. As we give thanks for the richness of these saving relationships, they can become icons to us – windows into the mystery of our relationship with God.

Deep in our subconscious we all have an archetypal father-figure. Even if we didn't have good fathering in infancy, we can learn to get in touch with that figure and build on the innate good feeling of 'Father' given us as part of our instinctual heritage.

We shall need to bring our painful memories, our wounds, our anger, our feelings of deprivation and rejection, for healing. Without healing of the memories we live with a massive block to growth and to our capacity to understand and enjoy this intimacy that God offers.

With the healing there may actually come the feeling of a bonus. The healed memories can transform our bitter experiences into a plus-quality. The psalmist knew something of this. He discovered God as his parent substitute:

> Though my father and mother forsake me:
> the *Lord* will take me up.
>
> (Ps 27:10 NTW)

Sometimes God reaches out in a deeper and *more* intimate way to those of his children who have been deprived and hurt. He 'restores the years that the locust has eaten', he fills up what has been lacking in our experience and gives us compensations for deprivations on the human level.

The maturing relationship with the Father

No relationship with a father remains at a level of childish prattle, however. There comes an enlarging of the innocent trust and unquestioning love. It has to mature into an adult bond with shared confidences and interdependence. It should lead to a growing mutuality. If it does not so develop, it will become trapped at a childish level and ultimately founder. Neither parental smothering nor infantile subservience will encourage fruitful dialogue.

Certainly Jesus opened up the possibility of a totally new intimacy with God by likening prayer to the trustful, open and innocent love of a child for his father. But that was only one side of the picture. From John's gospel in particular, we learn that it was not just to 'Father' that he prayed, but that it is the Father with whom he is one, the Father who sent him, the Father who works and whose work he shares.

This is a grown-up relationship – no longer the child pouring out his heart to his father, but the father speaking to and with his son. A mutual listening and receiving is involved. There is an entering in to the purpose of the Father, a cooperation with his will and a discovery of a oneness in the mutual exchange of trust and shared authority.

Prayer for Jesus was also 'Abba' at the level of an adult conversation between the Father and Son – an intimate conversation of shared secrets, a responsible one of shared purpose. His whole identity was wrapped up in this conversation. John shows us in his gospel that Jesus' self-consciousness was centred not in his ego (as ours so often is) but in the Father-Son relationship. His life had meaning only in so far as he was a response to his Father's will, a reflection of his Father's glory, an utterance of his Father's word, a baptism into the Father's heart of love, an all-consuming passion for union with the Father breathed out in a response of lovelonging and desire – a lovelonging which might have been expressed in thoughts similar to those of one of his saints, Isaac of Stella:

He himself is my contemplation;
He is my delight.
Him for his own sake
I seek above me.
From him himself
I feed within me.
He is the field
In which I labour.
He is the food
For which I labour.
He is my cause
He is my effect
He is my beginning
He is my end, without end.
He is for me
Eternity.[14]

4

'AS HIS CUSTOM WAS' – liturgical prayer

And he went to the synagogue, as his custom was, on the
sabbath day.

(Luke 4:16)

If the first prayer of the infant Jesus had been the prayer of
wonder, arising from sensitivity and awareness, the next step
would probably have followed shortly after. If it remains
a purely subjective thing, the inner, contemplative pull
common to many children can evaporate fairly quickly
with growing sophistication. It can die of inanition. It needs
to be harnessed, contained and encompassed within the
body of Christian prayer and given direction by objective
teaching.

The Jewish liturgical heritage

Brought up in a devout Jewish home with such godly parents,
Jesus would certainly have been introduced, at the earliest
possible age, to the liturgical heritage of his people. This gives
us a key not only to the prayers of the child Jesus, but also to
the pattern of prayer he would have observed throughout his
life.

In particular, since the three 'hours of prayer' were universally and strictly kept, we can assume with confidence that
they must have been part of the Lord's rule of life.

'As his custom was' (Luke 4:16) may refer to the predictability and structure of this aspect of his prayer life, as well as his habit of attending synagogue worship regularly.

In New Testament times the custom of praying three times a day had become a general rule (Acts 3:1; 10:3,30; *Didache* 8:3). In fact it was a practice that went back to pre-New Testament times. There are references to it in Daniel and Ezra.

Two disciplines were required of the pious Jew. He had, of obligation, to recite the *Shema* twice a day and to observe the three hours of prayer – in the morning, at three in the afternoon (the time of the afternoon sacrifice in the temple) and later in the evening towards sundown. The afternoon sacrifice is referred to in Ezra and Daniel as the 'evening sacrifice'. In Jerusalem the hour of sacrifice would be announced by a trumpet call. But while the worshippers and inhabitants of Jerusalem attended the sacrifice in the temple, the rest of Judaism was united to them in this act by praying at the same hour.

At each of the three hours, a Jew prayed the *Tephilla*, a hymn consisting of a number of benedictions – eighteen by the end of the first century. *Tephilla* really means 'grand benediction'. At the end of the hymn the worshipper was free to add his personal petitions. The normal, daily pattern would be to recite the *Shema* in the morning and evening and to follow it with the *Tephilla*. In the afternoon only the *Tephilla* would be prayed. The *Shema* was not itself a prayer – it was, and still is, a credal affirmation which was recited – and only by free men. Whereas the *Tephilla* consisted entirely of invocatory prayers and could be prayed by anyone – women, children and slaves as well as the men.

In addition to the three hours, there would be special benedictions before and after meals. Together these provided the basic rule and skeleton framework to ground and educate every Jew in the practice of prayer from childhood upwards. And of course this included Jesus. They were the rich legacy which he took with him into adult life.[1]

It was one thing to stop and pray the *Tephilla* at 3.00 p.m. while working in the carpenter's shop. How, we may wonder, did he manage it in his busy ministry? The professionals such as the Pharisees and the rabbis at Jerusalem could no doubt keep this rule of prayer without difficulty – even if they chose to go public on it! But how could a travelling rabbi, endlessly surrounded by people and bombarded by their demands, insist on breaking off to pray at the appointed hour? Jesus must frequently have been faced with the same dilemma that his ministers still face – the tension between the need for discipline *and* flexibility: the conflict of priorities.

Prayer and pastoral concern

When we begin to see prayer as 'a distilled awareness of our entire life before God',[2] we may feel that our availability to people in their need *is* our prayer at that moment. Occasions may arise when we decide that the most loving thing to do is to sit loose to structures and rules and give our total attention to others – to weep with those who weep and rejoice with those who rejoice. Jesus certainly knew that kind of prayer.

There is, however, the equally valid prayer of unavailability, and we know that Jesus was not afraid to offer that either, even at the risk of misunderstanding and disappointment. Sometimes it is actually more strengthening to others to withdraw and keep an appointment with God (for personal or, maybe, corporate prayer), than offer unlimited time and sympathy. It may, in the long run, be of more value to them to know that prayer takes precedence over everything else and is the essential source of any compassion we are able to offer. Indeed, it could perhaps suggest to them a way of seeking direct help from God which would lessen their dependence on human intermediaries.

Does it seem selfish to put prayer before the needs of others? Indeed, it *can* be selfish if wrongly motivated, as we know from Jesus' own story of the good Samaritan. But by far the greater danger seems to be the dispensing with commitment in order to be open and available to all whenever and for whatever. That way leads to ministry burnout. Perhaps we need to examine our motives fairly carefully. Are our deepest reasons those of concern for others, or those of self-interest . . . a need to be needed, a fear of creating a bad impression or a desire to give a good one? Have we developed a Messiah complex? Do we really believe we are indispensable? Are we hooked on success, even in pastoral care?

Perhaps it is a consolation to us to know that Jesus himself had to learn discernment – to safeguard the times of replenishment, to honour his prior commitment to prayer, not to allow himself to be at the mercy of every human need like a ship in a storm. He had to explain himself to his disciples at times when perhaps they might have thought him heartless. Sending them out on a mission, he instructed them not to try and convert the world but to set boundaries; to limit themselves to the house of Israel, not to try and reach the Gentiles and the Samaritans, too (Matt 10:5,6). He himself was prepared to follow the same precept in Canaanite territory – except that a woman of exceptional faith (and wit!) prevailed on him to heal her daughter. 'I was sent only to the lost sheep of the house of Israel', he said (Matt 15:24). But this was an occasion when he waived his rule in the face of a particular need and unusual faith (Matt 15:21–28). In doing so, he showed himself master of discernment and not slave to rigidity.

Those of us in Religious Communities who are also engaged in church work, with parish commitments, frequently find this difficulty when pastoral concerns conflict with the ordered Hours of the Religious Life. The saying of the Divine Office is part of the *raison d'être* of Communities. It is important, then, that absence from it should be with due discernment and not an indiscriminate erosion of a commitment. The same problem is posed to those in the ministry who undertake at their ordination to say Matins and Evensong each day or, in the case of Roman Catholics, to say their Office from the Breviary. For some this now raises great practical difficulties. Many are as faithful to this obligation as Religious who say the Office several times a day. And all the more credit to them, for it is infinitely more difficult to maintain this discipline individually and hiddenly than for those summoned by a bell to pray the Office corporately in monastery, convent or cathedral choir.

Jesus and corporate prayer

It could not have been any easier for Jesus to maintain a rhythm of liturgical prayer than it is for us. Yet, if he was true to his tradition, he did. Somehow he was able to observe the disciplines in spite of the pressures. Nor, one imagines, did he find it a burden. It would seem far more likely that it was a delight to him to punctuate his day with regular prayer in union with all devout Israelites. Did he, perhaps, find that the structures gave him freedom? Or, some might ask, did he find it cramping to be under obligation to say set prayers? Did they not become boringly repetitive? Certainly that is an objection raised about the Divine Office. 'Doesn't it all become very stereotyped and tedious?' people ask. But then non-liturgical prayer can also become very stereotyped despite the claim that spontaneity and flexibility give the Spirit greater freedom to blow where he wills. It seems that there is something in human nature that actually needs structure – even in prayer! Not a straitjacket, but something that sets us free from the burden of when, and how; something that enables our prayer to be like an arrow, effective and swift because direct. Prayer (whether extempore or not) that is without *any* shape or structure is rather like an amoeba which gets nowhere fast because it is too all-embracing.

We are wrong, however, to place liturgical prayer and personal prayer or extempore prayer over against each other. As with Jesus, the official prayer of the church is not an alternative to personal prayer; not instead of but in addition to; an enrichment rather than a deprivation. Jesus may have begun his solitary night vigils by reciting the *Shema* and saying the *Tephilla* before sinking into a deep, contemplative silence. And if at dawn he said them as the first of the three hours, they would vibrate with greater intensity for having grown out of his silence. He went away to pray at night, he arose early in the morning to pray. Do we see here one way in which Jesus maintained his rule of life? And do we also see something of the sacrifice involved?

There must have been, of course, great strength for him in the knowledge that he did not pray alone – that he was united with his fellow Jews in a common prayer. As true Israel, he had to be true *to* Israel. To pray in solidarity with others is supportive, encouraging and a stimulus to be faithful. There is the knowledge that the infidelity of one drags others down – like mountaineers roped together, if one slips, the others have to take the weight.

Familiarity with the mid-afternoon prayer can perhaps be seen from his parable of the two men who went up to pray in the temple – in all probability at three in the afternoon. Then, too, Jesus rebuked the Pharisees for parading their goodness by praying on the street corners (Matt 6:5). If they were out to get the greatest approbation from the largest audience, 3.00 p.m. would be the ideal time. When the loud trumpets sounded as a signal to the local people and visitors that this was the moment of the afternoon sacrifice, it was time for the devout Jew to stop, wherever he was, and pray the *Tephilla*. By some careful arrangement, it was quite possible for a Pharisee to find himself in a public place – the street corner or shopping precinct – at that precise moment and therefore 'forced' to pray in public and in full view of an admiring audience!

For Jesus it seems that the saying of the *Tephilla* provided a source of wealth which he was able to tap whenever he chose. In Mark 12:26 he speaks of God as the God of Abraham, the God of Isaac and the God of Jacob. Was this original, or was it a direct quotation from the first benediction of the *Tephilla*?

Blessed be thou, Lord (our God and the God of our fathers),
the God of Abraham, the God of Isaac and the God of Jacob
(God great, mighty and fearful,

most high God,
master of heaven and earth,
our shield and the shield of our fathers (our trust in every
    generation).
Blessed be thou, Lord, the shield of Abraham.[3]

His reference to God as 'Lord of heaven and earth' in
Matthew 11:25, is evidence of his *knowledge* of this particular
benediction of the *Tephilla*, even if it was not a direct
quotation. He may, of course, having been dipping into his
scriptural heritage, be remembering such verses as Exodus
3:6,15,16 and Gen 14:19,22, but these forms of address were
not currently in use in Judaism outside the *Tephilla* and they
are sufficiently similar to the words of the benediction to
suggest that it was this prayer that had been his inspiration.
Jesus was a radical. He introduced some disturbing
thoughts about interior obedience to the law. He blew apart
taboos that propped up externals in religion – and incurred
the wrath of the Pharisees whose prestige greatly depended
on these things (Matt 15:1–9; 23:1–36; Luke 11:37–54). But
we have no evidence that he dispensed with the disciplines of
liturgical prayer and public worship. He still acknowledged
his need to be a member of a worshipping community. Hence,
after his death and resurrection, his disciples were still to be
found in the temple 'at the hour of prayer' (Acts 3:1). They
continued to regard themselves as members of the Jewish
household of faith. It is highly unlikely that they would have
continued in this practice if Jesus had previously rejected it.
Only when incompatibilities became insurmountable was
there a breakaway from the Jewish tradition.

The value of liturgical prayer

Liturgy is a no-no word in some Christian groups. Perhaps,
especially among free churchmen, there is a fear of worship
becoming little more than something formal and dead. Certainly, it *can*. There is the risk of it developing into a valley of

dry bones – the skeleton is there, but no flesh and no life. It lacks the power of the Holy Spirit to quicken it into a living thing. The fact that formality and routine have sometimes killed it does not cancel out its value altogether. Each kind of prayer is open to its own particular dangers, but we do not throw prayer out in consequence. While recognising the danger of dead formalism, we can nevertheless appreciate the sheer objectivity of liturgical prayer. It purges prayer of undue subjectivism. It doesn't depend on *my* thoughts and personal inspiration. In liturgical prayer, we enter into the wisdom, beauty and riches of what has been prayerfully compiled under the guidance of the Spirit, and hallowed by use over a long period of time. It is one way of sharing in the communion of saints.

There is a right monotony in such prayer. The one-tone of it does away with the constant need for fresh ideas, novelty and excitement. It comes to our aid very especially in times of great spiritual darkness and aridity when we can dredge up *nothing* from inside ourselves. There is a givenness about liturgy which enables us to jump into the great river of prayer that flows ceaselessly to the Father and be carried along in it even when we don't *feel* like praying. The Spirit can give life and liberty to liturgy where the heart longs to pray. We may not *feel* excited, our minds may be distracted, it might seem dreary and rather pointless, but how it affects us is not important. In liturgy we are making an offering of prayer. In liturgy, Jesus made *his* offering; and the offering is all that matters, not whether we enjoy making the offering.

How can we possibly calculate the value to the world or the joy to God of a faithful company of men and women who face God as they get up in the morning, who continue to face him during the day and are still facing him when they go to bed at night? They are like the needle of a compass always pointing to the true pole of our being, counteracting the down-drag towards the pole of falsity and evil.

As we offer the official prayer of the church, whatever expression it may take in our tradition, we are joined to that faithful company of every age and race who have worshipped

God daily on behalf of the church and for the world – a company which included Jesus.

Liturgy is the divine wisdom dancing among men in the sight of God; it is the playtime of believers; it is a game with its own rules. As in any game, the purpose of the rules is to inspire and guide a shared creative effort, channelling it in a certain direction. Where, on the other hand, everything is done according to the book, play gives place to work-to-rule, and a very different atmosphere prevails. Only someone who has got the hang of the rules, and can consequently forget about them, is able to enter into the spirit of the game and abandon himself to the dance.[4]

5

'AS IT IS WRITTEN' – praying through the scriptures

As it is written, 'He gave them bread from heaven to eat.'
(John 6:31)

Anyone who has worshipped in a synagogue and noted the centrality of the scriptures and the priority given to them, the honour so clearly felt by those chosen to read and the reverence with which the scrolls, when carried round in procession, are touched by the congregation will be in no doubt that the Jews are a people of the word.

God is a speaking God. In the beginning, at creation, he spoke 'and it was done'. He spoke to Adam in the garden, to Abraham, calling him out of his comfort and wealth to be a sojourner, to Moses in the bush and on the mountain, to Elijah, to Samuel. 'The word of the Lord' came to each of the prophets commanding them to mediate that word to Israel, announcing, 'Thus says the Lord . . .' His word which went forth almost as an objective reality, a creative, dynamic word with a purpose, would not return 'empty'. It would accomplish whatever it was sent to do. He comes as the 'leaping Word'[1] into our midst. 'All things were lying in peace and silence, and night in her swift course was half spent, when the almighty Word leapt from thy royal throne in heaven . . .' (Wisdom of Solomon 18:14 NEB).

One of the saddest things about Israel was her inability to hear the word of the Lord (Isa 6:9,10). Her spiritual deafness led her into disobedience, for basically obedience has to do with hearing; (*ob-audire* – by hearing). The psalmist said, 'Sacrifice and offering you do not desire: but my *ears* you have marked for obedience' (Ps 40:6 NTW, italics mine). Mary's response of obedience was, 'let it be to me according to your word' (Luke 1:38). After toiling all night in vain, Peter's rather bewildered obedience to Jesus' instruction to cast the net on the other side of the boat to catch the fish was nevertheless given with, 'But at your word, I will . . .' (Luke 5:5).

For three hundred years the voice of prophecy had been silent. A faithful group – the *anawim* (the Hebrew word for 'poor') of whom Mary was one, together with Simeon and Anna – waited in expectation for that word which was to be their consolation.

And then, in the fullness of time, 'the Word became flesh' (John 1:14). Into the world and into human nature came 'Jesus of Nazareth, the Word with which God has broken his silence',[2] 'the word within a word, unable to speak a word, swaddled with darkness'.[3] He, the Word, warned men, 'Take heed then how you hear' (Luke 8:18). He said that his closest spiritual kinship was with those who 'hear the word of God and do it' (Luke 8:21). Receptivity to the word is a solemn responsibility. That becomes strikingly clear in the parable of the sower: 'He who has ears to hear, let him hear' tolls at its conclusion like a warning bell (Luke 8:4–8).

No one knew better than Jesus himself of God's communication through his word. He knew it very directly at his baptism and transfiguration – two decisive turning points in his ministry when the Father's voice was heard personally. But what Jesus heard on both occasions were key verses of the scriptures he already knew so well, brought together in a significant juxtaposition that gave fresh insight.

God often spoke to his Son in silence, through people, circumstances, the world of nature, the world of business, and through relationships; but undoubtedly, Jesus himself, within his own tradition, heard God speaking through the prophets, through the psalmists, in the law and the writings.

Through them he came to know more of his Father and of himself.

We can imagine him as a boy 'searching the scriptures' very eagerly, for they would minister to his deep and, as yet, inarticulate spiritual hunger. And, of course, his Jewish upbringing would ensure a familiarity with them. If liturgy was one part of a Jew's spiritual heritage, the scriptures were the other.

For those of us who are Gentiles, the novels of Chaim Potok (see Appendix) – set in the twentieth-century Hasidic community of Brooklyn – have illuminated for us something of the rigorous and exacting rabbinic training and discipline that orthodox Jewish schoolboys have to undergo in their study of the Torah and the Talmud in particular, and the Old Testament in general. But the law has always held a dominant place in the religious education of a Jew and the schooling of Jesus, in this respect, would assuredly have been thorough.

We can imagine the youthful Jesus avidly learning from his rabbi, memorising, assimilating, mulling over the mystery of the word handed down in this way. For whilst he *was* God's Word, he found his identity and vocation *through* God's word.

Mary was the space in which God became man, the silence in which his word could be heard, and the Jewish faith was the soil in which God chose to plant the seed of his Word, there to grow hiddenly at first before emerging into public view at the appointed time. Only so could the 'seed' grow naturally. For though the gospels say very little of those hidden years, nevertheless they give no hint of the young Jesus standing out from his peers as a religious freak.

The *anawim* had shown the deep piety, the unwavering faith and the goodness of which Judaism at its best is capable. Jesus showed forth the very best for, ultimately, he alone was true Israel. But, humanly speaking, he grew from the same soil as his godly forebears.

He fulfilled all the obligations of a member of the Jewish nation. He was a radical thinker, but not a marginal member. He probed to the roots and origins of his faith and tried to

recover integrity for some of its practices, not because he
devalued it, but because he was a faithful son of Abraham. He
was in a position to do so only by virtue of the fact that he had
not shunned the received traditions of his people. He was free
to jettison some of the unnecessary luggage accumulated
during their spiritual pilgrimage because he had allowed
himself to be bound by the essentials. He was happy to abide
by what was authentic in the religious observances of his day,
but, as we have seen, not content with pious practices alone.
Outward obedience was useless if it did not correspond to the
inner spirit.

Obedience to Jewish law and practice may have given him
the right to say certain things, but what was his real *authority*?
How did he distinguish the genuine, inner response from the
hypocritical 'front'? Did he rely solely on his extraordinary
powers of perception or upon his piercing ability to sift the
truth and go to the heart of matters? What gave him the right
to denounce the religious leaders, the professionals of his day,
as 'hypocrites' and 'blind guides'? His repeated, 'Woe to you,
scribes and Pharisees, hypocrites!' (Matt 23) was a shocking
indictment and an intolerable assault upon their self-esteem.
Jesus surely had to be very certain of his ground before
making such public attacks. But he *was* sure because,
anointed with the Spirit, he had been equipped with the gift of
discernment.

The evidence that we have in the gospels shows how again
and again he leaned upon the scriptures for his authority.
Surely not just scriptures as he had learnt them as a boy, or
even as he had listened to them read in the synagogue as an
adult, but scriptures which he had pondered at length, in
solitude and silence – the scriptures in which his life was
steeped and to which he listened with his spiritual antennae
fully extended, waiting for his Father to speak to him, disclos-
ing his will. His continual reference to scripture to support an
argument, to illuminate a truth, to point up a fallacy, to recall
a prophecy, to deepen understanding of God's nature and call
and to stir up hope, indicates something of the place the scriptures must have had in his prayer life as he exposed his whole

being to the word of God within them. They were indeed a lantern to his feet and a light to his path (cf. Ps 119:105).

Reading the gospels, we see how they interpreted for him his vocation, nourished his soul, were a defence in temptation and a cry in suffering; how he was immersed in them, enlivened by them, endued with the Spirit through them – and all from an early age.

Imagine his rabbi at school expounding the scriptures to him, opening up for him this vast treasure-store of his nation's wealth. It would have been meat and drink to the boy Jesus. They surely found in him not just an apt scholar, able to memorise and grasp them, but a mature, deeply-penetrating mind that could reflect and question and get to the nub of things, his whole spirit surrendering itself to the truth.

How else would a boy of twelve have impressed the learned teachers of the law to such an extent that they were unaware of the passage of time (Luke 2:41–51)? Must they not have been enjoying the cut and thrust of dialogue with such a young and unusually able thinker – someone whose insights challenged and surpassed their own?

Would that we had been told the areas in which he questioned the teachers! Was it perhaps the law? Had he already received something of a shock coming, as he did, from the atmosphere of Nazareth – the purity of his mother, the direct honesty of Joseph, the simple, holy rabbi, the unsophisticated life of a village – to this centre of worship where Jews gathered from throughout the Mediterranean world? Did he wonder at the religious 'show' put on by the professionals – publicly giving alms, praying where they could best be seen, announcing their piety by unwashed faces and dishevelled hair? He must, of course, have met deeply sincere Pharisees too, but did his ability to see through sham cause him to recoil at the others' apparent inconsistency in others between the spirit of the law and the practice of it? Maybe he couldn't help but be aware of the ulterior motives of those who sought honour, prestige, status and the praise of undiscerning people. He would not be the only child to have had this uncomfortably perceptive gift. Those who breathe pure air are more vulnerable to pollution, and worse affected by it, than those who breathe it all the time. Was this the experience of the young Son of God as he encountered the deadness of religious externalism?

Did he begin to discern, albeit dimly, even at this youthful age and in successive visits to Jerusalem over the years, how the law would have to be divested of the outward trappings and pettifogging minutiae, its hair-splitting arguments and absurd concentration on details, if it was again to be God's blessing to his people Israel? He who years hence was to say, 'you will know the truth, and the truth will make you free' (John 8:32) was perhaps deeply disturbed that the great law of Moses left people anything but free.

'Lord, how I love your law,' the psalmist had said (Ps 119:97 NTW); 'My delight shall be in your commandments which I have greatly loved' (Ps 119:47 NTW). In Jerusalem, however, the boy Jesus may well have been conscious of those who obediently declared their love for the law with their lips, but whose eyes told a different story – a story of defeat. People who, in truth, loathed the endless regulations introduced by the scribes that trapped them in wrongdoing whichever way they turned. Far from being a delight the law had become a heavy and impossible burden to the ordinary Jew. 'And his [God's] commandments are not burdensome,' said John (1 John 5:3). But they had become so for many in Israel.

We know that he grew to long that the law should not be destroyed but revived, obeyed in spirit rather than simply in letter, fulfilled – filled full with new meaning – by having the heart put back into it.

Or had his questions to the great teachers centred around 'the coming one' – the Messiah? Must he not have been very eager to learn more about the expected arrival of this saviour of his people? Would he be a leader like Moses with a special relationship with God? Would he be a king like David or a prophet like Elijah? Would he be able to hear God speaking to him individually, as Samuel did? Would he see visions in the same way as Daniel?

Most children identify with the heroes of their story books, or with TV personalities. Is it not likely that Jesus found himself identifying with the great figures of his race?

Probably he was particularly baffled by that enigmatic figure of the servant in Isaiah's prophecy. The suffering servant songs were like sea wrack washed up on the shore by the tide of prophecy and left there as a mystery to tantalise all until that time when they would find their fulfilment in the chosen one.

Meanwhile, who was the servant? Had he come and gone without being recognised? Had it been Jeremiah or Zerubbabel or Zechariah? Or was he still to come? To how many had the question been put, 'Are you he who should come? Or do we look for another?' Would the servant be an individual, a group of people or the whole nation of Israel? These were questions that many thinking Jews asked. In all likelihood, Jesus was one of them. As the years passed, would he have found himself dwelling rather more on these passages, meditating on them, absorbing their strange teaching of the servant whose mission would involve suffering and rejection? Did he so immerse himself in God's words to his servant that gradually he began to feel they were spoken to him personally?

These conjectures are more than vain imaginations, they are a holy wondering, a pondering these things in our hearts as Mary must have done.

'Is it safe to use one's imagination in this way?' some might wonder. Such spiritual masters as Teresa of Avila and St Ignatius of Loyola taught that it had a valid part to play in meditating upon the scriptures. Provided we bear in mind that conjecture, even if inspired, cannot be taught as gospel truth, we are safe.

What we know with certainty is that Jesus was developing a sense of identity. By the time he was twelve he already knew that he had come into this world with business to do – his Father's business (cf. Luke 2:49 AV). Quite what it was and how he was to set about it, was part of the reason for his long delay in the temple. This first visit to the central place of worship, and to the most important feast, had set in motion a whole train of thought which perhaps he had not been able to articulate before. Or maybe he had – possibly to his local rabbi who, finding himself somewhat out of his depth with this exceptionally gifted student, had prompted him to put some of his questions to the teachers of the law when he met them at Jerusalem.

We know the outcome of the story. With a new sense of the vocation in which he was to be engaged in his Father's business, he took the first step towards fulfilling it – obedience. Throughout his life the Father's business would be carried out so.

He did not stumble at the immediate hurdle which probably seemed so ordinary after the heights of vision. He went down to Nazareth with Mary and Joseph, submitting to their authority and, in so doing, grew in grace and stature and in favour with God and men.

Unquestionably he would have gone on pondering the scriptures for further clues about his Father's will for him. He would have reflected upon them with the same seriousness that an engineer studies a blueprint or a sea captain a navigational chart.

In his search for identity – the journey which we all have to undertake – would his heart not have resonated with the words of the psalmist as he prayed? Think how personally appropriate Jesus would have found the following verses, as he grew in understanding.

> How shall a young man's path be pure:
> unless he keep to your word? . . .
> O be bountiful to your servant that I may live:
> *in obedience to your word.*
> Take away the veil from my eyes:
> that I may see the wonders of your law . . .
> *I have more understanding than all my teachers*:
> for I study your commands . . .
> I have not turned aside from your judgements:

for you yourself are my teacher . . .
Through your precepts I get understanding:
therefore *I hate all lying ways.*
Your word is a lantern to my feet:
and a light to my path . . .
I am your servant, O give me understanding:
that I may know your commands.
It is time for the Lord to act:
for they violate your law . . .
I hate all lying ways.

((Excerpts from Ps 119 NTW, italics mine)

'It is time for the Lord to act . . .' How he must have felt the
truth of those words and longed to see just *how* God would
act. Perhaps he had already formed the habit of going out on
to the hillside to pray in solitude, long before he began his
public ministry. As the carpenter of Nazareth, did he reflect
on his own part in God's plan, and increasingly come to
realise that he would be part of God's action in response to
those who violated his law?

Was it not as a result of his meditation upon the scriptures
that he was able to discern when the time had come to leave
his workman's bench and quiet home life?

The authentic ring of the prophet's voice in his cousin, John
the Baptist, was like a clarion call to him. During that long
period when Israel had been without a prophet, they had
looked and waited for another Elijah who would be the 'voice
of one crying in the wilderness' (John 1:23), heralding the
Messiah.

Here, surely, *was* that Elijah, and his preaching was the
signal for Jesus to take the next step of obedience – an
identification with the current renewal movement among the
Jews, a movement of repentance symbolised in the rite of
baptism (previously only ever required of converts to the
Jewish faith).

In baptism, Jesus stood as one of, and with, his people.
Through it he showed his longing that Israel should be wholly
turned to God in a new conversion as radical as that of any

Gentile convert to the faith. But for him baptism and confirmation went together. His Father's voice, to which he had
learnt to listen through the scriptures from childhood, set the
seal on what he had done and the mission he was about to
begin. Through scripture his identity was affirmed by God
and, since he knew those scriptures so well, he grasped the full
implication of the divine utterance.

As he rose from the waters of the Jordan, a voice from
heaven said, 'This is my beloved Son, with whom I am well
pleased' (Matt 3:17).

> Highly significant words when we realize that they came
> from Ps.2.7 and Isa.42.1. One is the coronation formula of
> the Messianic King of Israel; the other the ordination
> formula of the Servant of the Lord. This remarkable com-
> bination cannot be fortuitous. It was his own destiny that
> Jesus saw in the Messianic King and the lowly Servant of
> the Lord. At his baptism Jesus was made aware that he was
> called of God to be the Servant Messiah, that he 'was born
> to suffer, born a king'.[4]

A suffering servant Messiah was an astonishing concept –
one wholly unacceptable and incomprehensible to Jews, as
Peter was later to show (Mark 8:32). Only the Lord's deep
acquaintance with the scriptures through study and meditation made it possible for him to receive these words as the
authentic voice of his Father. Only his previous reflection on
the inner meaning of the servant songs would enable him to
grasp their significance.

And after the baptism he was driven into the wilderness,
there to be tested. In the long period of prayer and fasting it
was scripture that armed him against the devil's attempts to
cast doubt on his newly confirmed divine sonship. To each
insidious attack of, '*If* you are the Son of God . . .', he
countered with, 'It is written . . .' His tempter, too, could use
scripture – for his own ends. Proof texts alone are never
enough – a prayerful understanding of the inner spirit of the
words is needed. Even though faced with hideous doubts and

choices, Jesus did not falter in his obedience for the Spirit of the Lord was upon him and had anointed him (cf. Luke 4:18).

The time came to share that knowledge as he expounded those very words in the synagogue. It was greeted with a storm of outrage. So it was to scripture that he turned for a title which would both hide and reveal his messianic identity. It would shield people from misunderstanding his role and from trying to acclaim him king, yet it would disclose his secret to the discerning. 'Son of man', therefore, became his enigmatic title.

Through the scriptures he discerned the nature of the work he must do. He was to be a second Adam restoring the free access to God that the first has lost; a second Moses with a new commandment, to 'love one another'; and a new covenant, not sealed in the blood of thousands of helpless animals, but in his own. He would be 'great David's greater Son' establishing a kingdom that would indeed be a theocracy. He would be a seer and declare the word of the Lord prophetically.

Prophet, priest, king, Son of man, servant, second Adam and second Moses – each aspect of his ministry grew clearer as he meditated upon these roles in the Old Testament. There in the scriptures he found his identity.

If, then, meditation upon the scriptures contributed to Jesus' understanding of who he was in God, it will be our experience too. Reflecting upon God's word in prayer, we shall be led more deeply into our understanding of what it means to be his child with the 'glorious liberty' that he delights to give to his children. We shall discover more of what it means to be a member of Christ's body – the church – with all the privileges and responsibilities that go with that membership. We shall deepen our understanding of the work of the Holy Spirit, the fruit of his indwelling and the particular gifts which he bestows – especially the ones he has bestowed on *us*.

There will be new insights about our relations with the world and the state. As citizens of the kingdom of heaven, we shall at times receive guidelines in the realm of ethics and

personal behaviour. We shall discover the kingdom, with all
its reversal of worldly standards, more demanding with every
passing day. We shall find that the Christian is called to a life
of paradox. We are to love, yet our love will bring judgment.
We are to make peace, yet disturb false peace. We are to be
law-abiding citizens, yet not of this world, for our citizenship
is in heaven. We are to obey the authorities (for all authority
is given by God) and yet identify with a revolutionary mani-
festo (Luke 1:51–53).

'Not the poverty of our own heart but the riches of the
Word of God must decide how we are to pray.'[5]

Praying the psalms

The chief way in which Jesus prayed through the scriptures
was, of course, through the psalter. It was the prayer book of
the Jewish people. He may not have had the benefit of
intercession leaflets, prayer letters or diocesan calendars, but
in using the psalms regularly he would have identified with the
whole range of human experience and emotion expressed in
them. They may not always have reflected his personal feelings or aspirations, but the Jew prayed not simply as an
individual but as part of the corporate body. Hence the
concept of corporate personality enabled Jesus to pray in
solidarity with his people.

He would have shared the psalmist's desire and longing for
God – with a uniquely poignant homesickness for heaven.

He would gladly have joined in expressing confidence in
God, acknowledging him to be a fortress, a tower, a high rock
. . . and all the other symbols of stability and strength.

He would have noted with joy the emphasis on the steadfast
love of the Lord which endures for ever.

He would empathise with the man who felt an outcast,
whose own familiar friend had betrayed him.

He would seek to enter into the cry of the man who felt cut
off, forsaken by God . . . a despised spectacle for the callous
passer-by to gawp at.

He would know the feeling of separation from a parent, as did the man whose mother and father had forsaken him.

He would enter into the pain of the wounded who called down curses on their enemies and persecutors.

He would be alongside those drowning in sorrow, in family or financial difficulties, in fear, self-disgust and shame as he prayed, 'Save me, O God: for the waters have come up even to my throat' (Ps 69:1 NTW).

He would surely love to sing of the time when all nations, kings and rulers would bow down before the Lord and submit to his supreme claims.

He would rejoice to praise God in the Hallel Psalms and delight to share in the psalmist's joy of the magnificence of creation and its power to dwarf man with his strutting, pompous little ego.

As for Jesus, so for us the psalter can provide fully comprehensive intercession material. We may be in the habit of praying the psalms as a way of praising God or expressing our longing for him, or of articulating our penitence. But, in fact, they cover even more than that. If we were to read through the psalter very slowly and jot down every different mood and aspect of life that it reflects, we should find it difficult to add anything to our list. The psalms voice the loftiest sentiments and the basest. They remind us of the young man whose path is pure and the one who has led a corrupt life. They speak of a longing for God and a longing for revenge.

If, like Jesus, we pray the full psalter regularly – a few psalms each day (not leaving out the unacceptable bits or putting them in brackets!), we shall stand as representatives of the whole of mankind. It is the prayer of humanity that comes before God in the psalms. *Someone, somewhere*, is feeling angry or hurt, full of revenge or full of wonder, needy and despised, exalted and blessed . . . and we pray with them and for them. Moreover, we pray in union with the Lord himself who hallowed the psalms by his own use of them.

'Only through daily use do we grow into that divine prayer book . . . anyone who has begun to pray the Psalter regularly and in earnest will soon have done with his own easy, "trifling, little devotions" . . ."[6]

The psalter filled the life of early Christendom. St Jerome tells us that in his days people could be heard 'singing the psalms in their fields and gardens'. When *we* soak ourselves in these ancient prayer songs, we too inherit the rich legacy which belonged to Jesus. And, of course, it was the words of psalmists which supplied his prayer in moments of crisis. So much were they part of him, they sprang naturally to his lips on the cross to express his sense of dereliction and his final commital.

Above all, just as they were a sure guide to Jesus, the scriptures will show *us* what it means to be obedient. There are times when we hear and know that the inner voice which speaks is that of the Father, but we are only disposed to recognise his voice on those occasions *because* we have been trained to hear it daily in his word. For meditation upon the scriptures in prayer is different from studying them as an academic exercise (although God can and frequently does speak to us when we are engaged in the discipline of academic study!). Reading the scriptures for purposes of spiritual reading and prayer, centres on internalising and personalising the passage, hearing it addressed to us *now*, asking what it is saying to us in our present situation, and what it is saying to us about the world. To do this effectively we should concentrate on short passages at a time. There is little value in rushing through long passages at great speed, and therefore very superficially. Nor does that kind of reading give due reverence to the living Word within the scriptures.

Monasticism from early days has called this kind of reading *lectio divina*. The purpose of lectio divina is to plant, water, nurture and bring to birth the Word within – for the Word is also to be found within our hearts. Dietrich Bonhoeffer once said 'just as you do not analyse the words of someone you love, but accept them as they are said to you, so accept the Word of Scripture and ponder it in your heart, as Mary did. That is all. That is meditation.' As the body abandons itself to the sun to enjoy its warmth without analysing the process scientifically, so meditation is a communing with God in abandonment – not an intellectual exercise.

Listening with the heart and entering in to the reality of which the words speak, we shall be brought into a living encounter with the Lord himself.

Meditation did not originally come from a word that meant to ponder or reflect. It meant to murmur persistently, praying a few words over and over again like Saint Francis of Assisi praying all night long 'My Lord and my God.' Cassian called it the 'rocking of the heart' which rises and falls rather like a ship dipping in the swell of the Spirit. So, in the rocking, the heart tumbles and turns the word of God until it has made it its own. A more contemporary and, I hope, not irreverent, image such as a tumble-drier might lend itself to help us grasp the original meaning of meditation. This is the kind of meditation which enables the word to take hold of us and to spring from our lips spontaneously as our own prayer in the same way as it did with Jesus.

In the Middle Ages, people used another apt and suggestive metaphor coming from the word *ruminari* which means to chew – in other words, to chew the word of God (As André Louf suggests in his book *Teach Us to Pray*)[7] like sleepy cows incessantly chewing the cud. It is a good picture. It speaks of tranquillity, of being totally engrossed, of patiently digesting . . . chewing, resting, regurgitating and chewing again. That is how the Word gets down into the system!

This is an important element in the prelude to prayer. The Word that I am turning over in my heart is, after all, no merely human word without life or lustre. It is God's Word, that is to say, it is a seed of life that can strike root and germinate; it is a glowing coal that purifies and gives warmth; a spark that can set my heart ablaze like a dry hay stack.[8]

The word that we chew has the power to fulfil the purpose for which it was sent, it has power to enliven, bringing about nothing less than rebirth and new life. There comes a moment of flashpoint when the Spirit in the word encounters the Spirit within our hearts, the one bearing witness with the other.

Even though limited, our experience of conceiving the word through scripture will perhaps throw light for us on the reason why Jesus had such a sure touch and perfect sense of timing in fulfilling his Father's will.

If we compare our experience to that of motherhood, first comes the conceiving of the word. We nurture it within us, as a mother-to-be nurtures the new life within her womb. We mother it, protect it, foster and feed it, allow it growing space. We listen to its heartbeat and its movements within, to what it is saying to us – indeed *demanding* of us and our obedience. And as we grow with it, changes take place in us. We find a new purpose in being, for we carry the word within.

But that is not all, of course. Like Mary, at the appointed time, we bring it forth to the world, holding out the word of life that has power to save.

Like Jeremiah, we know by the fire in our bones that we have no option but to speak forth the word. We cannot contain it any longer. The inner compulsion (perhaps to be compared to labour pains) means that the timing is right – the word will be set free to do its work and in due course to reap a harvest.

Obedience to that compulsion means that the word is spoken forth at the right moment and in the right situation, to disturb (as the prophets did), to command evil spirits (as Jesus and his disciples did), to rebuke (as Paul did in his 'severe letter'), to encourage (as Barnabas did), to share a vision (as John did from Patmos). It will be the word expounded and preached, but

preaching is a community business. It depends on all its hearers as well as its speaker. Indeed, a theology of preaching has to affirm that the preacher is not with the Word of God over against a congregation, but that preacher and congregation together are under the Word of God. Nevertheless, my experience is that there is rather

more blood, sweat, toil and tears preparing to preach a
sermon than preparing to hear one.[9]

There is that curious incident in the gospels when the
disciples come to the Lord and say, 'Your mother and your
brothers are standing outside (Luke 8:20). And he answers,
'Who is my mother . . . ?' (Matt 12:48). The answer: 'My
mother and my brothers are those who hear the word of God
and do it' (Luke 8:21).

We know, of course, that this was no slight upon his family.
Their appearance at that precise moment provided a good
opportunity to establish that the claims of the gospel took
precedence over all other claims, including those of the
family. The story has importance for us, too, because it tells
us that amazingly, we, too, are all invited to share in that
aspect of Mary's motherhood – whether we are male or
female, married or single, young or old. *We* are called to share
in that fruitful virginity, the singleness of heart which Paul
implied when he told his Christian flock that he would pray for
them 'till Christ be formed in you'.

We, like Mary, are called to be a hollowed-out space for the
word; called to be obedient to it; called to say, 'let it be to me
according to your word', called to be 'a silence in which his
Word may be heard'.[10] We can only fulfil this role of *mother-
ing the word* when we submit ourselves to it in humility and
receptivity, and, like Jesus, make it our inner prayer.

The problem for most of us is not in realising the importance of opening ourselves to the scriptures, of 'rocking' and
'chewing' the word, patiently digesting it and giving it space to
grow within us and bring forth fruit. It is finding the time and
the means of doing it. The mornings are so often a rush –
getting ourselves and the family off to work and school. In the
evenings we are tired and there is a meal to be prepared, a
meeting to attend or we are drawn by a good TV programme.
It is all very well to cite the practices of medieval monasticism,
but we don't live in that kind of world and they didn't face
some of the enticements of twentieth-century living.

The practice of making time to listen to God by dwelling

upon the scriptures has never, however, belonged exclusively to the monastic tradition (past or present). One has only to read the Puritan divines to discover how they were soaked in the word. Such books as the *Letters of Samuel Rutherford* have become classic spiritual reading because the author's knowledge of the word and deep love of the Lord warm and kindle our hearts like strong rays of the sun. The movements begun by John and Charles Wesley and George Whitefield, which set the country ablaze, were movements of the word. The great emphases of the Keswick movement on holiness and the Billy Graham campaigns upon conversion, arose out of devotion to the word. The 'Inner Light' of which George Fox used to speak was perhaps another way of expressing the idea of listening to the word within.

While *lectio divina* is the term used in the monastic tradition, 'the quiet time' is that usually used by evangelicals. And what a debt those of us brought up in this tradition owe to the stress laid upon the need for a regular time apart with the Lord to read and ponder his word and listen to his voice in and through it!

That 'quiet time' was sacrosanct and as much a norm in the daily programme as dressing and cleaning one's teeth. So too were family prayers. I can see my father now, with his well-worn copy of *Daily Light*, its pages crackling from long use in the damp, equatorial forests of Africa, reading to us and praying at the breakfast table before we began to eat. I remember that at summer schools, conferences, youth camps, and even staying with friends, trying to fit in the quiet time was not a problem.

It was catered for as an accepted part of the day, as it was too in our Missionary Training College. Various organisations within the church, such as the Christian Endeavour Society, Pathfinders, ISCF, Boys' and Girls' Brigades, and (for those in the Baptist church) the Girls' Auxiliary to the Baptist Missionary Society, encouraged young people to establish a regular devotional pattern as part of Christian discipleship and set for them a very demanding standard.

Of course it was costly at times, but the word, and relationship with the Lord through it, were part of the 'pearl of great price' for which we were prepared to sacrifice lesser pearls. No one who took the Christian life seriously would attempt to do without it. It was part of following in the footsteps of the master.

There were, and still are, a variety of aids to meditation in the form of Bible reading notes, which avoid wastage of time and energy and turn what might become a session of vague devotional mooning into a direct encounter with the living Lord through his word.

For some in today's world, the morning is not a realistic time for any quiet, and Breakfast TV may well compete for attention. The TV can become a very greedy master demanding our servitude all day and late into the evening. Has the quiet time suffered from this particular distraction? It would seem so, though it is not alone in claiming our allegiance.

At a time when I had a very busy teaching programme and rarely had an evening at home, I remember planning on one occasion to get my preparation and marking done before 9.00 p.m. so that I could watch TV. There was a film 'on the box' which I particularly wanted to see that night. I rushed through my work, bolted a hasty snack, and was just washing up in the kitchen with only a few minutes to go, when a voice spoke – so clearly that I gazed out into the blackness of the garden to see who was there.

I'm not given to hearing 'voices', but on this occasion it was so unmistakable that I looked for the owner of it. And the voice said, very gently and rather sadly, *'Could you not watch with me one hour?'* I was stunned. Needless to say the TV was not switched on. Instead, I went to my study and spent not one but two hours with the Lord in meditation upon the word and in prayer. And, in his incredible generosity, he gave great riches that night which were wholly undeserved in view of my initial reluctance.

The loss of the quiet time among today's believers is a terrible impoverishment. 'Don't let the world around you squeeze you into its own mould', said Paul (Rom 12:2 Phillips), but offer the spiritual service of worship which will lead to transformation and renewal of the mind, that we may prove what the will of God is.

'In order to experience the will of God, we need to give our *whole* lives as a living sacrifice [i.e. including our daily time-tables]. That means we detach our little cars for the merry-go-round platforms [of the world's way of living] and let God take us for a real ride.'[11]

> Every day look at the way you are living
> in the light of God's Word.
> Let it warm you when you are cold,
> encourage you when you are disappointed.
> You must not only be a hearer of the Word –
> you must also bring it to fulfilment.
> Happy are you if you meditate upon it
> daily in your heart:
> you will be like a tree by the running water,
> whose branches will stay fresh and green,
> and they will keep bringing forth new fruit.[12]

(See the Appendix for practical follow-up suggestions.)

6

'I HAVE PRAYED FOR YOU' – intercessory love

> Simon, Simon . . . I have prayed for you that your faith
> may not fail.
>
> (Luke 22:31,32)

Jesus' prayer for Peter

What must it have been like to hear the Lord himself say, 'I
have prayed for you'? Did this surprise Peter and the other
disciples? Were they aware that Jesus prayed for them –
individually and specifically, as well as collectively? 'Satan
demanded to have you, that he might sift you like wheat', is
spoken of all of them. The 'you' is plural. But, 'I have prayed
for you' is a word directly to Peter. The 'you' is singular.

Had Jesus referred on other occasions to his prayer of
intercession for them, or was the admission wrung out of him
at this point by the urgency of the situation?

These were his chosen disciples who had shared with him in
his public ministry, who had daily been in his company, seen
his signs and wonders, heard his teaching, watched people's
reactions to him. These were the hand-picked men he had
been carefully nurturing in faith and understanding so that the
kingdom might grow, spread and flourish from these small
beginnings. These were the ones in whom he had risked so
much and on whom the future church depended. Yet, in the
face of mounting hostility from official quarters, with an
imminent crisis approaching, they were wrangling about chief
places in the kingdom. He must have been grieved beyond

measure that here, at the eleventh hour, .they still hadn't grasped the essence of greatness. Perhaps he realised afresh, in this critical moment, just how frail were these men in whom he had invested his hopes, his teaching and his example. Taking a towel and a bowl of water he knelt before each one in turn, washing his feet, and demonstrating that greatness and humility are inseparable in the kingdom (John 13:3–5).

With his deep understanding of human nature, and the particular knowledge of each one that comes from love, he realised where the character flaws were, where the cracks would give way under pressure.

He could see Peter's particular weakness and knew just how vulnerable he was to temptation. So he prayed for him – that his faith would not fail, that he would not succumb to the cunning wiles of the Evil One.

He was concerned about Peter's *faith*. In the unedifying discussion which had just taken place, Peter had been rather too full of himself and his ability to cope. Jesus sensed a wrong self-confidence, an ominous streak of self-reliance that signalled danger ahead. For he knew Peter well. He was aware that, despite all the bombast, when it came to the test, Peter would crumple and collapse. His boast of being ready to go to prison and even die for his Lord had a hollow ring. It lacked the humility of one who knows perfectly well that he can do no such thing in his own strength. This was not the 'I can do all things *in him* [i.e. Christ] *who strengthens me*' of Paul (Phil 4:13).

So Jesus prayed that Peter should receive the gift of faith – not more strength, not more humility or a more realistic assessment of his capabilities. The stress is on fuelling a faith in danger of running out at the crucial moment, for it had been dangerously weakened by ambition. Faith would teach Peter trust – not in himself, but in God.

'When you have turned again, you will strengthen your brethen' (Luke 22:32). 'When you have turned again' implies repentance, conversion, facing in the right direction once more. Temporarily, Peter had been looking in the direction of power, honour and glory. He wasn't at that moment Peter, the Rock on which Christ could build. He had gone back to old patterns of thought, so is addressed as Simon. He was not being true either to himself or his vocation. Jesus is saying, in effect, 'When you have turned, when you have come to yourself, you will once more *be* yourself – the Rock, the support, the leader of your brethren.'

How must Peter have felt? How do we feel when someone says to us, 'I have prayed for you' – astonished, awed, grateful, privileged, unworthy, threatened? Wonder and gratitude are probably the chief feelings. But for Peter there must have been pain too. These words of Jesus contain a rebuke. He has pinpointed Peter's particular weakness – and mentioned it quite specifically – and has implied that Peter is not being his real self in all this concern about where he ranks in apostolic seniority and position.

It is said of Peter more than any of the other disciples that the Lord rebuked him, but here we have evidence that the rebuke was accompanied by, or in the context of, intercession. It is surely the 'I have prayed for you', that gives the authority to rebuke; the intercessory love that selects the words and manner of the rebuke – a salutary reminder to all of us!

The expressions of intercessory love

Were there other occasions when Jesus spoke of specific intercession? For whom else did he pray? He taught his followers to 'Love your enemies and pray for those who persecute you' (Matt 5:44), and we know that he did so himself: 'Father, forgive them; for they know not what they do' (Luke 23:34).

We are told that he spent a whole night in prayer before selecting his disciples. As he prayed around that choice, surely he would have prayed for each man individually?

In the same way, we could hardly imagine him healing the sick, forgiving the sinner and raising the dead without following them with his intercessory love. Nor if he had compassion on the crowds would he have neglected to lift them to God.

Intercessory prayer is more inclusive and all-embracing than articulated petitions, however. We may perhaps, at times, have viewed it too narrowly.

'To pray for others means to offer others a hospitable place where I can really listen to their needs and pains.'[1] Throughout his ministry Jesus was doing that – listening not simply to the words spoken such as, 'Have mercy on us, Son of David' (Matt 9:27) or 'I believe; help my unbelief!' (Mark 9:24), but also to people's movements, to the look in their eyes, the hopes and fears written on their faces. The whole of his sensitive being was constantly picking up the 'needs and pains' of others.

An intercessor is a mediator, and one of the chief things a mediator must be able to do is listen – to what is said, but equally to what is not said; to what is said through body language as much as through words.

A primary dimension of Christian prayer is receiving, is learning to listen. Listening is rare. There are certain people we meet to whom we feel we can talk because they have such a deep capacity for hearing; not hearing words only but hearing us as a person. They enable us to talk on a level which we have never before reached. They enable us to *be* as we have never been before. We shall never truly know ourselves unless we find people who can listen, who can enable us to emerge, to come out of ourselves, to discover who we are. We cannot discover ourselves by ourselves.[2]

What Edward Farrell says in these words could well be a description of how Jesus received people, gave them his attention, listened and heard them – really heard them, that is. And he enabled them to *be* as they had never been before. We know it was true of Zacchaeus, Mary Magdalene, the woman at the well, the woman taken in adultery, Nicodemus, Thomas (after the resurrection) and, of course, Peter (with his new name to mark the new being). But there must have been countless others among those whom he healed and taught who felt that in him their needs had been heard and met, and whose lives were, in consequence, radically changed.

In his listening he became the locus of encounter between God and others. In this sense he was a living intercession, for intercession is a prayer of meeting, of bringing two or more parties together for reconciliation, for healing, for mutual enjoyment. It is the prayer he continues to pray through believers today who seek to heal the rifts between opposing factions within the church or in society; those who work for the healing of broken marriages, split personalities, divided nations.

Compassion lies at the heart of intercession.

If I could have a gentle 'interiority' – a heart of flesh and not of stone, a room with some spots on which one might walk barefooted – then God and my fellow humans could meet each other there. Then the centre of my heart could become the place where God could hear the prayer for my neighbours and embrace them with his love.[3]

When we promise to pray for someone, how often do we truly enter into the reality of what that means? The story of the paralytic borne by four friends to Jesus for healing is a powerful illustration of intercessory love. We 'carry' those for whom we pray (we even speak sometimes of having 'a burden' in prayer). We bring them to the Lord that he may meet them in their need, touch their lives, restore their health and bring them the joy of his wholeness. Self is out of the picture, for we have become that other person experiencing his pain with him, suffering his fears for him, consumed with the same longings.

'Blessed are the merciful,' said Jesus (Matt 5:7). Part of the meaning of being merciful is to get inside the skin of someone else, to feel as he feels, think as he thinks, see as he sees, to understand life the way he understands it. That, of course, is at the heart of the incarnation. It is precisely what Jesus did when he 'got inside the skin' of a human being and experienced life as we do.

This kind of intercession is contemplative rather than petitionary. It is gathered up in compassion and empathy more often than words – though words are sometimes helpful to *us* in focusing on a particular person or need. We can bear people to the Lord, as the friends of the paralytic did, and leave them with him. We do not need to inform him of all the facts or suggest how he should act. We are not able to pray, but the Holy Spirit can pray through and in us. We cannot heal, but God can heal through us.

Intercessory love 'engages' the world to God, rather in the way that we engage the gears of a car to give it driving force. We 'enmesh' the two together in the silence of our hearts or in the groanings of the Spirit. But not, of course, without cost. For, entering into the sufferings of another is sometimes to have it round upon oneself. To 'carry' someone else can feel like a dead weight bringing great heaviness of soul. Nor are we always vouchsafed to see the results of having borne the load, as the words of this nun express clearly:

> There were days when the impossibility of seeing the result of one's prayer was disheartening almost to the point of faithlessness . . . one prayed for courage for those who had turned back upon the path, that they might turn again, but one's own body did not experience the shock of realisation, the reversal, the regathering of strength. One prayed for the faithless but it was not granted to one's ears to hear the crumbling of the walls and the shouting of the trumpet and the 'I believe . . .'[4]

The 'unknowing' may be hard at times, and merciful at others – for the knowledge of all would be beyond bearing. 'Now we see through a glass darkly.' Intercession has to be a mystery which confesses in love, for the moment I know only in part (cf. 1 Cor 13:12).

'I have prayed for you' applies to the registering of a need – the immediate concern we feel, the instant compassion or longing or anger. 'Whenever we remember another person in loving concern, we are praying for him.'[5]

To see intercession in this way removes unnecessary guilt if we have not been able to offer specific, verbal intention at the precise time requested. It means that the long list of requests for prayer does not become an impossible burden.

Rabbi Mendel of Vorki once said: 'The need of everyone leaves a trace in my heart. I open my heart and say, "Lord of the world, read what is written here."'

Intercession can be a form of ceaseless prayer, for when we invite the Lord to read what is written in our hearts, it will include everything that impinges on our consciousness. Our reactions of sorrow or joy, horror or delight – to a phone call, the news, a letter, a TV programme, a meeting with a friend, a meal with the family – all are open to his scrutiny. In intercession, the fragments of life are gathered up and nothing is lost.

If this is true of ordinary, sinful man, how much more must Jesus have lived his life as a 'distilled awareness'[6] before God. There may be few occasions when the gospel writers record him as actually saying, 'I have prayed for you'. There are many others when we are told he was moved with compassion. His look of understanding or pity for the despised or deprived, his sorrowful gaze upon Peter who had denied him, upon the rich young ruler unable to face the radical challenge of poverty, upon Jerusalem which did not know the things that belonged to her peace, were all part of his, 'I have prayed for you'.

His touch upon the untouchables, the blind, the lame, the deaf and dumb, the demoniacs and the dead were also part of his, 'I have prayed for you'. His tears as he watched over the city and wept at the tomb of Lazarus (and possibly on other occasions not recorded) were part of his intercessory prayer:

Copious tears and supplication for others mark the highest stage of perfect prayer . . . Our advancement in prayer, the gift of tears and true intimacy with God absolutely depend on our advancement in the ability to share with tormented and humiliated people. 'Remember those who are in prison, as though in prison with them; and those who are ill-treated, since you also are in the body' (Heb 13:3).[7]

His contemplative silence out on the hillsides was part of the same, 'I have prayed for you'. For 'it is in solitude that compassionate solidarity takes its shape'.[8] It is the eyes and ears that have been schooled in the desert of compassion that can take the raw material of what the media and everyday events offer and transmute them into intercessory love.

Without a certain element of solitude there can be no compassion because, when a man is lost in the wheels of a social machine he is no longer aware of human needs as a matter of personal responsibility. One can escape from men by plunging into the midst of a crowd![9]

Intercessory love depends, then, on a quality of seeing, of hearing, of being, for 'we don't just say prayers some of the time; we *are* prayer all of the time'. It demands a purity, for a mediator is a channel and a blocked channel is worse than useless; it fouls up everything and causes an obnoxious over-flow. Nor is intercessory love *purely* a matter of feelings and gut reactions in themselves. It is in partnership with Christ that we participate in the sufferings of others. It is the expression of an interdependence which he graciously ordains. Faithful intercessors become

true ambassadors for Christ on earth, reconciling men with God and God with men by means of their prayers, invo-cations and readiness to sacrifice themselves'.
    We do not obtain our partnership with the suffering, sick and humiliated people, nor can we bear the burdens of others, out of our own human affection, or from the spur of transient emotions, much less so from the desire to gain praise or for self-display – this type of sharing declines swiftly and finally disappears. But by persistence in pure, sincere prayer *we receive these feelings as a gift from God.*

This enables us not only to sustain but also to deepen our partnership with those who suffer, to a degree that we become unable to live without them and find no peace except in our sharing in their troubles and pains. The secret of this gift lies in our partnership with Christ and affinity with his divine nature and qualities in the sense that he himself is at work in us 'both to will and to work' (Phil 2:13).[10]

Jesus' high priestly prayer

In John 17 we are given the supreme example of Jesus' intercessory and priestly prayer for his disciples.

Firstly, he prayed that they might be kept from evil: 'Holy Father, keep them in thy name, which thou hast given me' (v. 11) '[I pray] . . . that thou shouldst keep them from the evil one' (v. 15).

By their very allegiance to Jesus they would be subject to the fiercest possible attack from the enemy, and the first way in which he would try to undermine their life and witness would be through division and party spirit. It has been his device in the church ever since.

So Jesus secondly prayed 'that they may be one, even as we are one' (vs 11,21).

In other words he prayed that the ceaseless love which flowed unhindered between the Father and Son should be the hallmark of their fellowship.

Thirdly he prayed that they might have the gift of joy: 'that they may have my joy fulfilled in themselves' (v. 13).

He had spoken of this joy before – a joy which had nothing to do with the fleeting, surface happiness which comes and goes. It was deep joy like an underground spring – there constantly as a source of life and refreshment; bubbling to the surface at times, at others flowing hiddenly. It is a given joy not dependent upon circumstances. It is *his* joy which will be filled full in them according to their capacity to receive it. (And strangely, most of us can cope with far less joy than suffering!)

His joy, of course, came from obedience to the will of his Father. Even the ultimate obedience could be described in terms of joy: 'looking to Jesus . . . who for the joy that was set before him endured the cross, despising the shame' (Heb 12:2). He wants that obedience to be the mainspring of joy for his disciples too. For that is the joy that will lead to glory. The greater the obedience, the greater the glory.

Fourthly, he prayed that they might be 'consecrated in truth' (v. 19): 'Sanctify them in the truth; thy word is truth' (v. 17).

Consecration is a setting apart for a particular purpose. The word has many sacrificial overtones. It was used in the Old Testament of setting things aside for a ritual purpose; once consecrated, they could never be taken back. It was used of setting aside people for special service. Jeremiah was consecrated before he was born (Jer 1:5). Aaron and his sons were anointed, ordained and consecrated as priests to serve the Lord (Exod 28:41). It is still used of church buildings and furnishings, eucharistic vessels, the consecration of bread and wine, of bishops, of members of Religious Orders when they take life vows. But when it is *people* who are set apart, they are also equipped by consecration with the qualities of heart, mind and character necessary for the task.

Here Jesus prayed that the entire life of each disciple might be 'made holy to the Lord' (as the priest was holy to God – Lev 21:6), that he might be set apart by and for the truth, consecrated to the word – to proclaim it, teach it, immerse himself in it. For their sakes he, Jesus, would consecrate himself 'that they also may be consecrated in truth' (v. 19). They, in turn, would learn what it meant to consecrate themselves, to be separated and holy, for the sake of the world, the flock of God, the sheep they were commissioned to feed, the sheep which were 'not of this fold', i.e. Gentiles.

To be consecrated for the word, by truth, to holiness, *for the sake of others*, is the prayer of Jesus which we can still pray with him. For Jesus continues, 'I do not pray for these only, but also for those who believe in me through their word' (v. 20).

Looking to the time when the 'mustard seed' of the kingdom would grow through the ministry of these men, Jesus prayed for all who would come to believe 'through their word'.

Did he foresee some of the problems the church would have to face in learning to open its door to 'all nations', in integrating those from other faiths and cultures, in living harmoniously together while respecting widely differing temperamental needs?

Whatever the full import of this prayer, there is no doubt about his desire and will for unity: firstly, because through it they would enter into and reflect the loving unity of the Father's relationship with the Son.

Secondly, he prayed that they might be one for the sake of the world – 'that the world may believe' (v. 21) – that no competition, exclusiveness or quarrelling should frustrate the free course of the gospel, and no division within the church weaken her evangelistic impact. 'A divided world will give little heed to the voice of a divided Church.'[11]

Thirdly, he prayed for unity so that they might 'be with him': 'Father, I desire that they also, whom thou hast given me, may be with me where I am, to behold my glory . . .' (v. 24).

Here his prayer links with his previous exhortation to the disciples: 'Abide in me, and I in you. As the branch cannot bear fruit by itself, unless it abides in the vine, neither can you, unless you abide in me' (John 15:4). 'To be with him' was not merely a prayer for the life beyond this life, for a share in the heavenly glory, but for a living relationship with him here and now. It is the 'in Christ' of Paul's epistles, a deeply personal bond in which his life would continually flow into them as the sap of the vine flows through all its branches. Without that close union there could be no possibility of growth or fruit.

Finally, he prayed that they might be full of love, 'that the love with which thou hast loved me may be in them, and I in them' (v. 26).

The whole of this chapter of John's gospel could be covered

by the words 'I have prayed for you.' It is Christ's prayer for
his disciples and his church, with its solemn and awesome
challenge. He prays for them: protection from evil, a ceaseless flow of love, joy through obedience, consecration, unity
leading to effective witness, a living relationship with and
total dependence on him, and, again and above all, love, a
love such as exists between the Father and the Son.

Jesus' continuing intercession

So, returning to the question with which we opened this
chapter, what must it have been like for Peter to hear the Lord
himself say to him personally, 'I have prayed for you'? We *can*
still hear him say those words, for 'he always lives to make
intercession' (Heb 7:25). He continues this high priestly work
for all time, praying these same things for his church today;
praying for us individually that our faith shall not fail in
temptation, that we shall be 'turned' again and again in
conversion when we have taken refuge in our false selves and
plunged headlong into darkness rather than walking in the
truth. He still prays that we shall be 'with him', in a deep,
unique relationship, sharing in his mission, sharing in his care
of the poor and oppressed, sharing in his desire for liberation
and justice for all men, sharing in his passion, consecrated to
the truth, abiding in him.

'He [Jesus] holds his priesthood permanently, because he
continues for ever. Consequently he is able for all time to save
those who draw near to God through him, since he always
lives to make intercession for them' (Heb 7:24,25).

Since it is his continuing intercessory work, and since he has
invited us to share in this mystery which transcends human
intellect, sanctifies human feelings and becomes a source of
healing and power for others; since he has entrusted to us his
heart of love and a share in his compassion, we must echo
Samuel's words: 'far be it from me that I should sin against the
Lord by ceasing to pray for you' (1 Sam 12:23).

7

'GLORIFY YOUR NAME' – powerful prayer

'Father, glorify thy name'. Then a voice came from heaven,
'I have glorified it, and I will glorify it again.'

(John 12:28)

If we wanted to find the unifying principle in the life of Jesus, and indeed his life's prayer, we have it in these words. To glorify God was his ceaseless aspiration. Everything he did, said and was became a love-offering to the Father to bring glory to his name. Is it surprising, then, that he should have wanted that to be the end and aim of all his followers? 'Let your light so shine before men, that they may see your good works, and *glorify your Father* which is in heaven' (Matt 5:16 AV).

What it means to glorify God's name

But what does it mean to glorify the Father? What did it mean to him as he prayed these words? How can we pray them with him?

The desire for God's glory was the dominant factor in Jesus' life; his whole being was consistently directed towards it. How can our desires become unified and our energies harnessed in that one direction? Our multifarious desires often conflict, and our preoccupation with self takes up so much energy. Yet if this is Jesus' *raison d'être*, then surely should it not be ours?

'Father, glorify thy name . . .' To the Jew, the name

conveyed the character and personality of the one who bore it. It *was* the person. When Jesus said 'I have come in my Father's name' (John 5:43), it meant he had come with his Father's character and personality. When, for example, he taught his disciples to say, 'Hallowed be your name' or when the law said, 'You shall not take the name of the Lord your God in vain' (Exod 20:7), it had little to do with the profane use many make of that name when it becomes part of a vocabulary of swear words. (That is not to say that we should feebly tolerate the offensive and pathetic practice of using God's name to relieve hurt feelings or express annoyance at some trivial inconvenience!)

To glorify God's name was to glorify all that he was and all that he had done, to glorify his will and purpose, to glorify what he had created and established. That was how the Jew saw it. The name enveloped the whole divine being. By praying as he did, Jesus made it abundantly plain that his sole desire – not only on this occasion, but throughout his life – was that God's will should be done, God's character should be seen, God's love should be made available and accessible.

In the Old Testament, those who profaned the holy name were those who did *not* reflect God's nature and character, who contravened his laws, who lived unethically, who were merciless and cruel, sexually immoral and unjust. We have only to read Amos' searing indictment of the rich to see this.

Amos launched a blistering attack on those who cheerfully celebrated the feasts and proclaimed the fasts at the right time, who maintained an outward show of piety and yet cheated their neighbours by falsifying the weights on the scales, who robbed the poor man of his last hope of getting out of debt by selling him and his family into slavery, who idly lolled about on ivory couches in the luxury of their town houses or country seats, who enjoyed exotic food and wine and drank from silver goblets while the needy went hungry and homeless at their gates, were crushed and oppressed and finally sold as slaves dirt-cheap – for the price of a pair of shoes (see Amos 2:6, 7; 3:15; 5:12; 6:4, 6; 8:4, 6).

Along with other Old Testament prophets, Amos pointed

out that to live lives that ignored the ethical, political, moral and social demands of God was to *desecrate* his name, no matter how piously it was called upon in private prayer or public worship. The smoke of burnt offerings and sacrifices made by such people positively stank in God's nostrils. God asks for 'faithful love . . . not sacrifice', Hosea said, 'knowledge of God [i.e. an understanding of his character], not burnt offerings' (Hosea 6:6 NJB).

We hear Jesus echoing this teaching to the Pharisees: 'Go and learn what this means, "I desire mercy, and not sacrifice." For I came not to call the righteous, but sinners' (Matt 9:13). It also finds a place in what he had to say about the final judgment. It will not be those who have dutifully called 'Lord, Lord', who will necessarily find themselves in the kingdom (Matt 7:21) – not if their lives have been inconsistent with the profession of their lips – but those who have shown mercy to the hungry, the thirsty, the stranger, the prisoner (Matt 25:31–46). Such people have glorified God by their active compassion, even if they weren't aware of it.

By healing the sick and feeding the hungry, by casting out demons and cleansing lepers, by accepting the outcast and forgiving the sinner, by condemning self-righteousness and pious humbug and by lifting up the penitent, by identifying with the poor and exposing the corruption in the corridors of power, Jesus was glorifying the name of his Father.

When the Jews came to him and said, 'How long will you keep us in suspense? If you are the Christ, tell us plainly,' Jesus replied, 'I told you, and you do not believe. The works that I do *in my Father's name*, they bear witness to me' (John 10:24,25). Works done in the Father's name were to be the clue to his identity. For him the prayer of glorifying God found its expression in his constant disclosure and unfolding of the true nature of God. He said in astonishment to Philip, 'He who has seen me has seen the Father; how can you say, "Show us the Father"?' (John 14:9).

When Mary sang of the mighty Lord who had done great things for her, she declared, 'holy is his name' (Luke 1:49) and then explained why, and in what way, that name was holy –

because the Lord had 'scattered the proud in the imagination of their hearts, he had put down the mighty from their thrones, and exalted those of low degree; he had filled the hungry with good things, and the rich he has sent empty away' (Luke 1:51–53).

Translated into contemporary terms, where do we see God's name being glorified today? In every move towards justice and human rights; in every attempt, individual or corporate, to achieve a fairer distribution of the world's resources and a right ecological balance; in every effort to provide shelter for the homeless and beauty for the inner city; in every overture towards an alienated party or desire for true reconciliation, whether it be between nations, tribes, colours, creeds or partners within a marriage or whether it be negotiating the release of hostages or resolving an industrial dispute.

It is in Mother Teresa and Bob Geldof, Terry Waite and Desmond Tutu that we see God's name being glorified . . . and in countless others who, in sacrificial ways that never make the news headlines, are reflecting God's passion for justice, peace and love, and thereby reveal his nature. 'By this my Father is glorified, that you bear much fruit', said Jesus (John 15:8).

There is no escaping the fact, then, that glorifying the name is a matter of holy lives rather than holy words. And yet we cannot leave it there. Social action is not all that there is to glory.

How Jesus glorified the Father

The context in which Jesus often spoke of glorifying the name of the Father was that of obedience to the Father's will. His whole life had been an ongoing process of *learning* obedience – through submission to the law and the ritual requirements of the Jewish religion, to his family and teachers, to the disciplines of his trade, to his own growing sense of vocation. Faithful at every point during his years of seclusion, he was ready for his public ministry and the obedience that would be learnt through suffering (Heb 5:8). So unfalteringly had he revealed the character of God from his birth onwards – indeed from conception, for even at that stage the fullness of the Godhead had dwelt in him bodily (Col 2:9) – he could say, 'He who has seen me has seen the Father' (John 14:9).

His ministry began with obedient submission to the voice at his baptism which ordained him and set him apart to suffer (Matt 3:17). Even when Peter remonstrated with him and showed him the absurdity of such an idea (this must have seemed to Jesus as though he were back in the wilderness being tempted to believe that he could fulfil his messianic vocation without suffering) he remained obedient to his insight and heavenly intuition (Matt 16:21–23). As he rebuked Peter (Matt 16:23), he must surely have recalled and been strengthened by those words in Isaiah's prophecy: 'You are my servant . . . in whom I will be glorified' (Isa 49:3).

When the excited crowds, so recently and miraculously fed, would have hailed him as a king, he resolutely turned away from the temptation to seize that kind of power and dismissed them (John 6:15; Mark 6:45).

Obediently he followed the path of inexorable suffering. And while the conflict with his enemies intensified as, again and again, they tried to establish his disobedience to the law and even to Caesar, he was given further confirmation by the Father that he had understood his mission aright.

At the transfiguration the voice was heard again, 'This is my beloved Son, with whom I am well pleased; listen to him' (Matt 17:5), and Moses and Elijah, representatives of the law and the prophets, spoke to him of his exodus, his departure (Luke 9:31). He received this renewed commission as he moved towards the final crisis and with it the manifestation of the glory which was with him.

He didn't go up to the city dragging his heels reluctantly, although he must have had a clear idea of the probable consequences of such a journey. He went up still hungering for the will of God – almost in love with it. Not abandoned to it in resignation, which is the lowest form of obedience, but 'in an active quest to penetrate further into it'.[1] It was his meat to

do the will of him who sent him and to accomplish his work
(John 4:34). His obedience was the outcome not only of love,
but of trust, and, as Susan Lenkes says,

> Stoop-shouldered,
> foot-dragging
> sighing
> resignation
> is
> not
> trust.
> Real trust
> bounces on eager toes of
> anticipation –
> laughs with the
> pure delight of
> knowing
> in whom
> it believes . . .[2]

Now came the final step. It was within the context of a
lifetime's obedience in every respect that he could face his
'hour'. 'Now is my soul troubled,' he said (John 12:27).
He knew that he was approaching the climax to which his
whole ministry had been pointing and the destiny which had
determined the course of his life.

He could not escape the knowledge that his hour would
bring confrontation with all manner of evil and, therefore,
inevitable suffering. Part of him quite naturally shrank from
it. So what was he to say? 'Father, save me from this hour'?
Answering his own question he responded, 'No, for this
purpose I have come to this hour'. He had faced his 'hour' in
anticipation many times before. But now it was about to
become present reality. The wilderness temptation to look for
an escape from the suffering presented itself again. There was
only one prayer that would save him from retreat. As the
'interior struggle between human shrinking and spiritual
willingness to fulfil his vocation'[3] waged within him, back

came that 'ceaseless prayer of aspiration',[4] 'Father, glorify your name.' And with this fresh utterance of the prayer which had formed the basis of his entire life, came the Father's immediate response, 'I have glorified it, and I will glorify it again' (John 12:28). With the successive victories of obedience, God could count on Jesus for this final one – the one on which the whole salvation plan hung. For it was the total offering of a life of complete obedience from beginning to end – not just a sacrificial death – that would restore the broken relationship between God and man; there were no failures anywhere along the line.

To pray the prayer of Jesus, 'Father, glorify thy name,' is an acknowledgment that nothing less than total obedience will do. It expresses the desire to reveal God's character and obey his will. But, of course, it is beyond the power of any of us to be totally obedient. We are all born with that rebellious streak called original sin. We are like a weighted wood in a game of bowls which cannot but go out of the true.

Was it, then, any easier for Jesus, who knew no sin (Heb 4:15), to offer this life-prayer? It is true that the more habitual sin becomes, the easier it becomes. Consciences grow sluggish and habit-tracks of disobedience are formed from which it is hard to break free. Yet we have to be careful about diminishing, even by suggestion, the genuine struggle and choices Jesus had to make. He was not programmed like an automaton so that he *could not* disobey. Every act of obedience was a response of the will, not a conditioned reflex. Undoubtedly every victory made the next one more assured. But we need to acknowledge the reverse side of the coin – which we know from our own more limited experience. The more we resist the Evil One, the more insistent are his pressures, the more insidious and frequent are his attacks. The struggle actually becomes fiercer and the onslaught more continual. 'Not uncommonly, those most pure are prey to the least avowable temptations.'[5]

Sometimes, when a reigning world boxing champion climbs into the ring, his fans chant, 'Easy, easy!' expecting that he will demolish his opponent in a few rounds.

We need to beware of building up an image of Jesus in which he is a 'star' for whom the fight is easy. He was the proper man, but not Superman; perfectly obedient, but not effortlessly so. The writer to the Hebrews is quite explicit about the cost and anguish involved in his obedience: 'In the days of his flesh, Jesus offered up prayers and supplications, with loud cries and tears' (Heb 5:7).

It was still an agonising struggle for Jesus to pray in Gethsemane 'nevertheless not my will, but thine, be done' (Luke 22:42). First he had cried out, 'Father, if thou art willing, remove this cup from me'. But it was not to be removed, so there came the response, 'nevertheless not my will . . .' Yet the acceptance did not bring automatic or immediate calm. Luke tells us that, 'being in an agony *he prayed more earnestly*' (v. 44).

We know in our own experience how the initial 'Yes' to God in obedience, our 'Thy will be done' in a situation where what is asked of us goes against the grain of all our natural inclinations, does not mean the battle is over. We have to go on saying the 'Yes' at deeper and deeper levels as we wrestle with the implications of that obedience.

You dare your Yes – and experience a meaning.
You repeat your Yes – and all things acquire a meaning
When everything has a meaning, how can you live
    anything but a Yes[6]

Think what those implications were for Jesus at this point! And *yet* his prayer was 'Father, glorify thy name.' He had a mission to fulfil – a mission which would glorify his Father when it was accomplished . . . in the Father's way. 'I glorified thee on earth, having accomplished the work which thou gavest me to do' (John 17:4). And having been 'obedient unto death' (Phil 2:8), he could cry from the cross, 'It is accomplished' (John 19:30 NEB).

It was a mission accomplished in his incarnate body. Paul sees how it is continued in his mystical body – the church:

Blessed be the God and Father of our Lord Jesus Christ, who has blessed us in Christ with every spiritual blessing . . . In him, *according to the purpose of him who accomplishes all things* according to the counsel of his will, we who first hoped in Christ have been destined and appointed *to live for the praise of his glory*.

(Eph 1:3,11,12)

For Jesus, the prayer 'Father, glorify thy name' led to suffering and death – an ignominious, shameful, humiliating death by which he mysteriously glorified God. We must not be surprised if when we pray the same prayer it involves us in suffering too – the suffering of a daily dying to those things in our lives which are not 'according to the purpose of him who accomplishes all things according to the counsel of his will'.

For the early church it often meant literal, physical suffering – even to martyrdom. So the writer of the first epistle of Peter warns his flock not to be taken by surprise when the fiery ordeal comes upon them, 'But rejoice', he says, 'in so far as *you share Christ's sufferings*, that you may also rejoice and be glad when *his glory is revealed* . . . if one suffers as a Christian, let him not be ashamed, but under that name let him glorify God' (1 Pet 4:13–16). (Peter himself had been warned by Jesus of the suffering that lay ahead: 'This he [Jesus] said to show by what death he [Peter] was to glorify God' (John 21:19).)

Suffering and glory go together in the New Testament. It is the Christian conviction that the Christian will share *all* the experiences of Christ. 'If we suffer, we shall also reign with him' (2 Tim 2:12 av).

Jesus actually spoke of his death in terms of glorifying the Father and the Father glorifying the Son. 'Father, the hour has come; glorify thy Son that the Son may glorify thee' (John 17:1).

But, of course, the Father was glorified not only in the life and death of his Son but also in his resurrection and ascension. To glorify the Father is to know not only the fellowship of Christ's sufferings but also the power of his resurrection; to enter deeply into the passion but to explode with new life as the Easter people; to share Christ's body and live his risen life; to drink his cup and bring life to others. It is to rejoice in Christ's exaltation; for having glorified the Father through his obedience, the Father does indeed glorify the Son: 'Jesus . . . emptied himself, taking the form of a servant . . . he humbled himself and became obedient unto death, even death on a cross. Therefore God has highly exalted him' (Phil 2:5–9).

No wonder when Pilate said, 'Behold, the man!', 'the whole of Christendom has shouted back for two thousand years, "No! Behold your God!" '[7]

To make 'Father, glorify thy name' one's ceaseless prayer, as Jesus did, and to be consumed with a passion for God's glory is eventually to be filled with that same glory. Hence Jesus could pray, in his prayer for the church, 'The glory which thou hast given me I have given to them' (John 17:22).

God gives his glory

Originally God gave his glory to his whole people, Israel. He appeared in a cloud – the Shekinah glory. It was the sign of his presence among them. It led them through the wilderness; it stood over the tent of meeting; it came to rest more permanently in the most holy place. Yet more than once the glory left them.

In the wilderness they forsook God and changed their glory into the golden image of a calf (Ps 106:20).

When Eli's daughter-in-law was about to give birth, she received news that her husband had been killed and the ark of God had been captured. She did not call her child Phinehas, after his dead father, but gave him the name *Ichabod*, meaning *'The glory has departed from Israel'* (1 Sam 4:19–22).

In a vision, Ezekiel the prophet saw the glory of the Lord departing from the temple – driven out by the idolatry and faithlessness of Israel (Ezek 10). The connection of God's presence with the sanctuary was severed for the exiles who were deported to Babylon. But later in his prophecy comes the vision of a new Israel purged of her apostasy to alien powers, with hearts 'sprinkled clean' (Ezek 36:25; Heb 10:22), the covenant renewed and her vocation embraced afresh. He saw a restored temple, perfect in every dimension and detail, becoming once more the habitation of God's glory. God would again take up residence in the temple of his people, Israel.

'As the glory of the Lord entered the temple by the gate facing east, the Spirit lifted me up, and brought me into the inner court; and behold, the glory of the Lord filled the temple.' And a voice said, 'Son of man, this is the place . . . where I will dwell in the midst of the people of Israel for ever. And *the house of Israel shall no more defile my holy name*' (Ezek 43:4,5,7). There follows a list of the specific ways in which Israel had previously defiled God's name through all sorts of abominations.

Martin Buber tells us that many Hebrews think of God's glory as still wandering on the face of the earth looking for its ark or dwelling place. He says, 'Pray continually for God's glory that it may be redeemed from its exile.' He points to the teaching of the Kabbala (a system of Jewish theosophy believed to reveal to its initiates hidden doctrines) in which it is one of the basic conceptions that 'the Shekinah, the exiled glory of God, wanders endlessly, separated from her "lord" and that she will be reunited with him only in the hour of redemption'. The solitaries who wander over the earth 'to suffer exile with the Shekinah' nevertheless recognise 'moments in which they see the Shekinah face to face in human form'.[8]

The Christian believes, of course, that God's glory *has* been redeemed from exile, that the new life of communion with the holy God to which Ezekiel's imagery pointed has broken upon us. He believes that a *new* temple 'makes possible that fellowship between God and man which can never again be imperilled'[9] – a temple made not with human hands, but flesh. Through the one who was true Israel, God has returned to the midst of his people to take possession of them.

'The Word became flesh and dwelt (lit. tabernacled or

tented) among us . . . we have beheld his glory' (John 1:14). We do indeed 'see the Shekinah face to face in human form', for the light of the knowledge of the glory of God has shone in the face of Jesus Christ (2 Cor 4:6). In him the glory has been 'reunited with her Lord at the hour of redemption'.

Malachi also saw the Lord returning to his temple – suddenly. 'Behold, I send my messenger to prepare the way before me, and the Lord whom you seek will suddenly come to his temple' (Mal 3:1).

He returned in the temple of his incarnate body (his own description of it – John 2:19). His glory continues among men in his body the church – not just the establishment, the hierarchy, etc., but in the inner shrines of all who make up that body.

With the prophecies of Ezekiel and Malachi in mind, Charles Wesley could pray for divine love to visit us with salvation and enter every trembling heart,

> Suddenly return, and never,
> Never more thy temples leave.[10]

God's transforming and transfiguring glory

When we long for God's glory – passionately – he comes to light up his house (every receptive heart) with his own glory. As we face towards him 'beholding the glory of the Lord', we are 'being changed into his likeness from one degree of glory to another' (2 Cor 3:18).

That process of change will come through openness to God in prayer and sacrament, in receptivity to the word. It was *while* Jesus was praying that he was transfigured. That great mystery took place as he was looking at God, open to God, in prayer. And his disciples who were awake and praying saw the amazing and awesome sight. In Gethsemane, when they were asleep instead of watching and praying, they missed the angel who came to strengthen Jesus. But on the mount, when they were with him in prayer, like him open to God, they were awake to reality – the greatest reality they had ever encountered.[11] Here, a human form was bathed in a glory which radiated from him in dazzling brightness. Here they saw man as he was meant to be, for Irenaeus claimed that, 'the glory of God is a man fully alive'. 'Hence, when we lovingly gaze at the face of Jesus Christ in frequent prayer that has no other motive than the glorification of God, the mental veil is lifted from our spirits and we perceive the glory of God's nature in Christ "who has shone in our hearts".'[12]

Peter's instinct was to build something quickly – more tabernacles – to capture the moment and house the glory, to localise it as previously it had been enshrined in the ark and the earthly temple. But Jesus didn't respond to the suggestion. From now on the glory is not to be given a fixed, material abode but to be set free to shine forth in and through human personality – dazzling, attracting, terrifying.

When we meet truly holy and deeply prayerful people, isn't it true that we often sense a luminous, shining quality about them – hard to describe yet quite remarkable? We sometimes speak of the aura that surrounds them. In their presence we feel deeply in touch with reality. They have about them the glow of transfiguration.

A young landlord, Nicolas Motovilov, sought out Saint Seraphim of Zarov, whose reputation had spread far and wide as a healer. After being healed completely of his paralysis, he continued to visit the Staretz.[13] He recounts one occasion when he witnessed a transfiguration experience of the saint.

I looked and was seized by holy fear. Imagine in the middle of the sun, dazzling in the brilliance of its noontide rays, the face of the man who is speaking to you. You can see the movement of his lips, the changing expression of his eyes, you can hear his voice, you can feel his hands holding you by the shoulders, but you can see neither his hands nor his body – nothing except the blaze of light which shines around, lighting up with its brilliance the snow-covered meadow, and the snowflakes which fall unceasingly.[14]

How are we to understand this account in terms of our own experience? Are we to expect that the deeper we go into prayer, the longer we are in the path leading to holiness, the more we shall develop a dazzling quality? Will *our* faces shine with glory? The answer, amazingly, is 'Yes.' As A. M. Allchin has said, 'when the Holy Spirit touches the whole of a man, energising and transforming his life at every level, a wonderful radiance of glory is released'. He goes on to claim that 'the light of God shines out through the very body of the one who has died with Christ'.[15]

Certainly there are those of us who can testify to having seen a face transfigured in death. In *The Hiding Place*,[16] Corrie ten Boom speaks of the miraculous transformation of her sister Betsy who had died in the prison hospital of Ravensbruck an emaciated, pale, drawn and prematurely aged woman. When she found her sister had gone from her ward, Corrie was distraught but, astonishingly, one of the nurses called her to the mortuary to look upon the beautiful, fleshed-out body of her sister, her hair restored to its normal colour, the lines of the face smoothed out and giving way to an expression of deep peace. Perhaps that was exceptional, and yet does it perhaps happen more frequently than we realise – simply because we don't have the opportunity to see this glory?

A former infirmarian of our community told me of an occasion after a sister had died when for some reason it was necessary just before the funeral to open the coffin. The doctor was present and as the lid was removed they gasped aloud. The body of the sister was radiant with a translucent light which completely transformed her body. We can't explain why this happens, we only know that there is evidence that sometimes it does in those who have lived lives of holiness and prayer.[17]

It is not only in death, however, that we have evidence of such glorious light – as Nicolas Motovilov bears out. In fact most of us are more familiar with the story of Moses and how after a period of intense communion with God *his* face shone causing great fear to his people – a holy, wondering fear (Exod 34:29,30).

Surely we have all known a human face transfigured by intense joy? Is it not true that most brides look beautiful – not simply because of the bridal dress, the special hair-do and careful make-up, but because of the deep, inner joy that shines out? They are radiant from the inside!

Or it may be the shining eyes of proud parents as they gaze in wonder at the wriggling scrap, with puckered, red face, that is their first-born child.

Or, later, it may be their faces shining with pride as they watch their offspring receiving honours at a prize-giving ceremony.

These are instances of natural joy. But have we not also seen the 'shining' in the faces of those alight with the experience of conversion or renewal in the Spirit, or in those about to make their profession of faith and public avowal to the Lord in baptism?

We may not have seen transfiguration in quite the way that Nicolas Motovilov describes it, but we all must surely have seen it. If not in this shining quality, then perhaps in another way.

Metropolitan Anthony Bloom once described two icons of the transfiguration which struck him very deeply when he saw them in the original in the Tetriakov Gallery in Moscow. One is by Rublev, the famous iconographer. The other is by his master, Theophan the Greek.

In both there are three mountain peaks, the Lord Jesus in the centre, with Moses and Elijah on the right and left-hand sides, and the three disciples on the slopes of the mountain. The difference between the two icons lies in the way in which things are seen. The Rublev icon shows Christ in the brilliancy of his dazzling white robes which cast light on everything around. This light falls on the disciples, on the mountains and the stones, on every blade of grass. Within this light, which is the divine splendour – the divine glory, the light itself inseparable from God – all things acquire an intensity of being which they could not have otherwise; in it they attain a fullness of reality which they can have only in God. The other icon is more difficult to perceive in reproduction. The background is silvery and appears grey. The robes of Christ are silvery, with blue shades, and the rays of light falling around are also white, silvery and blue. Everything gives an impression of much less intensity. Then we discover that all these rays of light falling from the divine presence and touching the things which surround the transfigured Christ do not give relief but give transparency to things. One has the impression that these rays of divine light touch things and sink into them, penetrate them, touch something within them so that from the core of these things, of all things created, the same light reflects and shines back, as though the divine life quickens the capabilities, the potentialities of all things, and makes all reach out towards itself.[18]

So then, the light of transfiguration may be seen as either shining *out* or shining *in* to make all things transparent. It is a penetrating quality, an ability to see to the very heart of things, to behold the inner beauty of what may outwardly be esteemed ugly, to marvel at the hidden goodness lying at the heart of a sinner, to discover the saint in disguise. It is akin to the Spirit's gift of discernment. It is to be possessed oneself of a transparency, of becoming what man was originally intended to be.

Have you ever wondered what we should have been like but for Adam and all that followed on from original disobedience? Surely we are given our greatest clue in the transfiguration of Jesus, where we see a human being filled with the light of God's glory and glimpse how it might have been for us all. There we see what should have been the norm for humanity.

An orthodox hymn expresses very beautifully how, far from being a sad reminder of our sub-normal, sinful state, the transfiguration points the way to 'shining again' through the work of redemption.

A revelation of our true humanity

He who once spoke through symbols to Moses on
  Mount Sinai,
Saying, 'I am he who is',
Was transfigured today upon Mount Tabor before
  the disciples;
And in his own person he showed them the nature of
  man,
Arrayed in the original beauty of the image.

Having gone up the mountain, O Christ, with thy
  disciples,
Transfigured thou hast made our human nature,
Grown dark in Adam, to shine again as lightning,
Transforming it into the glory and splendour of thine
  own divinity.[19]

From time to time we are privileged to meet those saints who through their deep prayer and close walk with the Lord 'shine again as lightning'. They have become men and women 'wrapped in light as in a garment' (Ps 104:2 NTW) and living temples to God's glory.

Almighty Father,
whose Son was revealed in majesty
  before he suffered death upon the cross:
give us faith to perceive his glory,
that we may be strengthened to suffer with him
and be changed into his likeness, from glory to glory.[20]

'FATHER, FORGIVE THEM' – redemptive prayer

And Jesus said, 'Father, forgive them; for they know not
what they do.'

(Luke 23:34)

Almost anyone, believer or not, knows that Jesus prayed
these words as he was about to be crucified. That in itself is
significant. They are so astonishing that they have captured
universal wonder. At times we might even be tempted to wish
that they were not so well known, so hard are they to follow
and so powerfully do they accuse us when we fail to forgive.
Yet, in this, of all the prayers that he prayed, we come close to
the heart of Jesus, the man of prayer.

The context of Jesus' prayer of forgiveness

The circumstances in which this prayer was offered are
so familiar there is a danger they might cease to make their
full impact. Christians are sometimes criticised for an over-
concentration on the passion of Christ. It is probably truer to
say that, individually at any rate, we are not concerned
enough. Overfamiliarity with the facts has made us casual.

In crucifixion the cross was laid flat on the ground. Jesus
would have been stretched upon it and ten-inch long spikes
driven into his wrists and ankle bones. If that was not pain
beyond the threshold of most human beings, there had
already been the scourging, one of the cruellest punishments

ever devised. The pieces of bone and lead with which the cords of the whip were studded tore a man's back to ribbons. Besides this, he had stood for the long hours of his trial without food or drink. On to his sore and bleeding back had been loaded, none too gently we can be sure, the heavy, wooden cross. No wonder he stumbled under its weight. In those conditions many men would have died before reaching the place of execution.

It was the practice, after the nailing, for the cross to be raised and dropped into a socket in the earth with a great thud which jolted the victim terribly as his pinioned hands and feet took the full weight of the body.

It was a hideous, obscene form of execution. In the world of that day none was more agonising and long drawn out. Yet it was as the hardened Roman soldiers hurled Jesus on to the cross and began their nailing without any ado (no chaplain, no dignified rituals, no final word of consolation, no farewell or last wishes, not a trace of human kindness or even pity) that Jesus prayed these words, 'Father, forgive them . . .'

What *must* the soldiers have thought? Curses and oaths they expected and probably got frequently; but a prayer for forgiveness must have been totally outside their experience. Did it soften them at all? It is perfectly true – they *didn't* know what they were doing. They were like pawns in a game of chess being used to seize the king. They probably had no qualms about their role, it was all in a day's work to them. But later on – would the words of this prayer have lingered to haunt and puzzle, driving them to search for meaning to this extraordinary death? It was probably the first time, in all their experience of dealing with criminals, that they had met someone who loved his enemies and prayed for those who despitefully used him. They were unaware that they were witnesses of the greatest spiritual conflict ever waged. Here love incarnate fought out the final battle with evil . . . and conquered.

Pain and forgiveness

When we pause to consider what pain does to most of us, and our reactions to it, don't we have to admit that it *can* bring out a rather ignoble side of our characters? We become absorbed in our pain, we whine for sympathy, complain bitterly, grow full of self-pity and rage. Whether or not it is a physical ailment or wounded sensitivity, hurt body or hurt feelings, we can all fall prey to the 'poor little me' syndrome. And we won't leave the raw places to heal. We worry at them like a dog with a bone, refusing to let them go, all the while growing increasingly unhappy. Somehow the pain which fills our horizon leaves us isolated since it does not feature so importantly for others and their patience soon wears thin.

When it comes to the pain of injustice, misunderstanding and humiliation, the natural reaction is to strike back, to hurt – if not the offender, then whoever happens to be conveniently around on to whom therefore we can project our anger.

On the other hand this kind of pain can be the means of calling forth a reaction that is far more than natural. It is supernatural, because it is love. This is what the soldiers unwittingly witnessed. They saw a love which could disregard pain and go out undiminished towards the perpetrator of the evil – a love which is the principal ingredient of forgiveness.

> Forgiveness is specifically a matter of dealing with pain . . . Forgiveness describes the positive, redemptive response to pain, in which, for love's sake, the hurt is contained by refusal to return it with anger and in which love and goodwill are maintained unbroken towards the offender . . . The original hurt is isolated and so, being contained within the hurt person, is not instrumental in bringing about an increase in the total amount of pain and a consequent proliferation of evil . . . [When] the supernatural will to love has become entirely dominant over the natural will to take revenge the pain is absorbed – redeemed – in the hurt person and healing flows from that person to the

original offender. A pain has been transformed by grace into a source of love for both people.[1]

Some of the greatest examples of this kind of supernatural response to pain have come out of the concentration camps of World War II, where men and women in extreme suffering discovered something of the spirit of Jesus and were able to share in his prayer, 'Father, forgive them . . .', the prayer which lives on in the body of Christ wherever he continues to be betrayed, humiliated and tortured.

The cell was a concrete box too narrow to sit down in. One could only bend one's knees a little so that they were thrust up against the door, and the position becomes so agonising that it is hard not to cry out. In the end, after hours have passed, one subsides into a state of constant whimpering . . . To pray in such circumstances is not easy, but it is great and sweet solace if one can do so, and one must try with all one's strength to love more, not less. I had a struggle not to sink below the level of love and fall back into the realms of hatred, anger and revenge; to love Romulus Luca (the prison guard) not for a moment but continuously. I had to drive my soul to do this as one may push a vehicle with locked brakes. It was now that I came to understand Luca, his blindness and narrow hatred, his reactions which were like those of a dog rendered savage by being chained too long, or of a slave put in charge of slaves, with no freedom except to torment them. And then my thoughts went to those . . . whom it was natural and easy to love. I found that now I loved them differently, now that I had learned to love Luca; I came back to them as though from a distant place. And it was in that cell, my legs sticky with filth, that I at last came to understand the divinity of Jesus Christ, the most divine of all men, the one who had most deeply and intensely loved . . .[2]

So wrote Petru Dumitriu in his autobiographical novel *Incognito*.

It is a mystery how such appalling experiences should reveal the sense and meaning of the universe to those so brutally treated. But it is the testimony of a not inconsiderable number. Humiliated till they were meant to feel less than human, they actually discovered some of the greatest spiritual truths. Petru Dumitriu continued, 'Why had I expected the world to justify itself to me, and prove its meaning and purity? It was for me to justify the world by loving and forgiving it, to discover its meaning through love, to purify it through forgiveness.'[3]

In the passion of Jesus, the cruelty of the soldiers, the hatred and scheming devices of the religious leaders, the moral cowardice of Pilate, the betrayal of Judas, the denial of Peter and the desertion by all the disciples had combined to set loose upon the world a great tidal wave of evil. Such things always do. It has been released again in our own age in the Holocaust, in Siberia, in Japanese prisoner-of-war camps, El Salvador, Robben Island, Argentina, Chile; in the inner cities of Western Society, in the increasing number of homes where little children are beaten, starved and tortured by their own parents. For whether it is Belsen or Brixton, the mass graves of Auschwitz or the tiny grave of a battered baby, it is the same evil.

Forgiveness, on the other hand, releases a power that can only be described as spiritually therapeutic. (It is sometimes physically so, too! Consider, for example, how many people have let go their resentments and found their arthritis practically gone. We are such psychosomatic beings our physical disorders often have related emotional causes.) Think, too, of the marriages healed through forgiveness, the churches united through mutual forgiveness, the friendships remade through forgiveness.

Love . . . is most significantly the pain-bearer . . . it does not yield to those reactions by which evil is caused to proliferate, and thus it is the entire underlying principle of forgiveness. But . . . it is even more: for if pain is robbed of its power to provoke evil in a viciously proliferating circle, and if love rules the reactions to it, then the evil one has been defeated at the heart of his strategy.[4]

If we can see the healing effects of forgiveness even in our limited experiences, how much more amazing is this prayer of Jesus which indeed defeated the evil one 'at the heart of his strategy'?

Pain in itself is morally neutral. It is how it is used that either sets free a great healing river or lets loose a destructive force far worse than any poison-gas leak or nuclear explosion.

'Forgiveness is the crowning accomplishment of love, both in God and men.'[5] On the cross we see 'the love that never faltered, the love that paid the price';[6] a love which enabled Jesus to pray, 'Father, forgive them . . .' It introduced the most dynamic energy this world has ever known – an energy that could explode out of a sealed tomb. When this same energy is appropriated by men it empowers *them* to look up and see the glory through the wounds. Pain is transfigured into an agent of redemption.

When Jesus prayed 'Father, forgive them', it was not simply an appropriate or pious expression, something he felt was expected of him in the situation. He was not even consciously putting into practice what he had preached. He really *wanted* forgiveness for his tormentors.

Praying for forgiveness

For us the prayer of forgiveness is often the hardest to pray when others have hurt us. But it is absolutely obligatory – that is, if we wish to receive forgiveness ourselves. Yet it must not be prayed with that attitude of self-concern uppermost in our minds either. It is the overflow of a disinterested love. But do we really take this injunction of the gospels seriously? We know it with our heads, but our hearts are slow to follow. We may bring ourselves to pray that the one who has offended us should be forgiven. We may have *said* that we forgive them, from the bottom of our hearts. And we meant it. But, oh dear!

the next offence committed by the same person . . . and it seems that far from having forgiven, we have only buried the grudge and temporarily forgotten the pain. Given half a chance it all comes surging back. It is one thing to forgive seventy times seven different offences; it is another thing to have to go on forgiving the same injury 490 times simply because the wound in us will not heal. Yet there can be no doubt about Jesus' condemnation of smouldering anger that cannot forgive. Letting go and setting free are the inner realities of forgiveness. As we let go of the grudges and the wounds, we set free both the offender and ourselves.[7]

It is precisely for this reason, i.e. our inability to forgive totally, that we need to meditate often on the passion and to hear that redemptive prayer of forgiveness said for all time and for us personally. 'Father, forgive them' that they seem unable to forgive.

How well Jesus understood our human frailty when he told the parable of the unjust steward (Matt 18:23–35). He who had received so much mercy himself was unable to forgive his fellow servant a comparatively trifling debt. Rather he cast him into prison. That is when we get a vivid picture of what God's righteous anger at the hardness of men's hearts is like.

How different from the woman who came to pour her costly gift of perfume over Jesus, and of whom he declared, 'Therefore I tell you, her sins which are many, are forgiven, for she loved much; but he who is forgiven little, loves little' (Luke 7:47 RSV).

God takes this matter of praying for forgiveness very seriously. The capacity to pray in this way is what makes us priests, following in the footsteps of our great high priest, pleading for mercy for those who need it.

In Isaiah 59:1–16 we are given a picture of a society which could easily be our own. It speaks of 'hands defiled with blood', lips that 'have spoken lies', tongues that have muttered wickedness. No one goes to law honestly, 'their feet run to evil', 'they make haste to shed innocent blood', 'destruction and desolation are in their highways', 'the way of peace they know not', 'there is no justice' but 'oppression and revolt', 'truth has fallen in the public squares and uprightness cannot enter', etc.

And we are told, 'The Lord saw it, and it displeased him . . . He saw that there was no man, and wondered that there was no one to intercede'. He was amazed that no one had been sufficiently concerned to stand before him as priest and intercessor and plead mercy for these benighted people heading for their own destruction.

He invites us to participate with him in this priestly work by praying 'Father, forgive them', not simply because of our own injured feelings and battered pride, but on behalf of those who flagrantly defy God's laws and have no intention of asking for forgiveness. We are called to stand on the Godward side of the evildoers.

Standing in the gap

When we see on our TV screens the artist's impression of a man wanted for abducting a child or shooting the cashier in a Sub Post Office, what emotions are stirred? A desire for revenge? Waves of sympathy for the relatives? A sick feeling at the increasing violence in our society? A longing for justice and humankindness? Maybe a mixture of them all? But do we pray 'Father, forgive him', opening up a channel for God's redemptive power to reach him? Does it make *us* turn to God in penitence and confession for all the seeds of that same violence which lurk in our own hearts – oh yes, carefully held in check by our social upbringing, conditioning and, maybe, religious training, but nevertheless *there*? It should. There is a purity needed for the work of intercession. Nowhere is this more clearly expressed than in the Lord's promise to Solomon after the dedication of the temple as the house consecrated to the praise of his glory. He said, 'if my people who are called by my name humble themselves, and pray and seek my face, and turn from their wicked ways, then I will hear from heaven, and will forgive their sin and heal their land' (2 Chron 7:14).

Moses exercised that priestly calling when, in horror at the incident of the golden calf, he pleaded with God to spare his people. 'Alas, this people have sinned a great sin . . . But now, if thou wilt forgive their sin – and if not, blot me, I pray thee, out of thy book which thou hast written' (Exod 32:32). The psalmist, speaking of this prayer of Moses, says that God would have destroyed the people 'had not Moses his chosen stood before him in the gap: to turn away his wrathful indignation, lest he should destroy them' (Ps 106:23 Coverdale).

'Standing in the gap' is a mediatorial work. The mediator is one who stands between two parties representing the one to the other. Here Moses stood as one of and with his people, identifying with their sin, offering his life as atonement for it. But he also stood as God's man to his people declaring God's law, mercy, love and forgiveness.

Paul made a similar offer: 'For I could wish that I myself were accursed and cut off from Christ for the sake of my brethren' (Rom 9:3). He was prepared to stand in the gap if, by doing so, enlightenment could come to his own race.

One of the most significant verses of the New Testament is Mark 10:45: 'The Son of man also came . . . to give his life as a ransom for many.'

The offers that Moses and Paul made to give their lives 'as a ransom for many' were not accepted. That highest mediatorial work was left for Jesus alone. Quite literally, he stood in the gap – fixed between earth and heaven, between man and God, where in a 'deep and mysterious way, he entered into the collective unconscious of the human race. There he took into himself all the violence, all the fear, all the sin of all the past, all the present and all the future. This was his highest and most holy work.'[8]

'MY GOD, WHY HAVE YOU FORSAKEN ME?' –
the prayer of desolation

Forsaken! First by his followers and now seemingly by God. He is abandoned – and we all fear abandonment. It haunts our nightmares. We try to grasp the fear and reduce it to manageable proportions by articulating it in story form: legends and myths frequently take the 'lost and found' theme. The abandoned child or the abandoned dog stir in us compassion and, in the process, allow a shadow of fear to fall across our minds again.

Jesus' experience of forsakenness

Abandonment by parents and friends is terrible enough, but abandonment by God is ultimate forsakenness. It is hell. So Jesus cries 'Why?' Why has he been cut off, abandoned, plunged into an abyss of horror and aloneness?

Two things may be noted here. Firstly, Jesus is praying from the scriptures, as he so often did, this time from Psalm 22:1. Could it have been that this cry of dereliction was wrung out of him as he recalled that the scriptures also said, 'a hanged man is accursed of God' (Deut 21:23)?

Just as the Hebrews laid their hands upon the scapegoat imputing to it their sin, and then sent it off into the desert, abandoning it to die, so he had been taken 'outside the camp' (Heb 13:11–13) and left to die without human or divine support. Worse, the full weight of the world's sin, the whole 'cosmic havoc'[1] created by man, the sum of all the disorder and dis-ease within society throughout history had been imputed to him, the divine scapegoat.

We who are sinners know times when we feel our sin to be grievous, the burden of it intolerable. Confession is the gift given to us to lay down the burden, to be set free from the guilt. *How* must it have been for the pure Son of God who had shunned sin in every guise throughout his life, who had never borne guilt, nor known the feeling of shame . . . What was it like to take the full weight of the guilt, the shame of all men?

Sometimes we block our ears and cry, 'Don't tell me any more. I can't bear it,' when someone recounts a particularly horrible story of human cruelty. Jesus had no such protection or immunity from the full impact of evil. And the only one in a position to help him bear the unbearable seemed to have deserted him. Furthermore, if he was *accursed* then he was, by definition, beyond the reach of God, for the accursed man or thing could not come in contact with the holy God.

We can only have a mere glimpse of what that must have meant to the Son who had been one with his Father throughout his life. However horrendous his physical agonies, the agony of not being able to feel consciously that communion with the Father, his Father's power flowing through him freely, the certainty that his Father was operating through him now, must have been the crowning torment. Utter darkness.

The second thing to note is that he did not for one minute fail in obedience, yet he dared to ask 'Why?' He did not curse God like his neighbour on the cross. But he questioned him. And that is consolation indeed to those of us who have cried out 'Why?' in the moments when we have felt abandoned and cut off from God. Not that our experiences – even the sum total of them – could compare with the desolation that Jesus felt. The closer you are to anyone, the more terrible the separation is. But we are permitted to share in small ways in the darkness that Jesus knew. And it is *all right* to ask, 'Why?' Jesus' cry, 'Why have you forsaken me?' at least implies the possibility of someone being there. Teresa of Avila was a very forthright, no-nonsense type of woman, and, on one occasion when she had felt God's absence in a particularly painful experience, she turned to him afterwards and said, 'Well! Where were you in all that?' And the Lord replied, very graciously, 'I was there all the time.'

Our experience of darkness

Just as we know that 'in Christ God was reconciling the world to himself' (2 Cor 5:19) and not actually absent, even though Jesus' feelings of abandonment were genuine, so we can know that in our experiences of darkness and desolation, he has not left us utterly. Nevertheless, we shall experience the darkness as terrible. We, too, will find ourselves asking 'Why? What is the purpose of it, if any?' C. S. Lewis certainly did:

Meanwhile, where is God? This is one of the most disquieting symptoms. When you are happy, so happy that you have no sense of needing Him, so happy that you are tempted to feel His claims upon you as an interruption, if you remember yourself and turn to Him with gratitude and praise, you will be – or so it feels – welcomed with open arms. But go to Him when your need is desperate, when all other help is vain, and what do you find? A door slammed in your face, and a sound of bolting and double bolting on the inside. After that, silence. You may as well turn away. The longer you wait, the more emphatic the silence will become. There are no lights in the windows. It might be an empty house. Was it ever inhabited? It seemed so once. And that seeming was as strong as this. What can this mean? Why is He so present a commander in our time of prosperity and so very absent a help in time of trouble?

I tried to put some of these thoughts to C. this afternoon. He reminded me that the same thing seems to have happened to Christ: 'Why has thou forsaken me?' I know. Does that make it easier to understand?[2]

We cannot fathom the mystery of God's seeming absence entirely, but we begin to learn that in prayer it is increasingly difficult to distinguish between God's presence and God's absence. When he *seems* most far away he is often closest to us – so close that he is out of focus.

Nevertheless, since we are all called in some way to share in this experience of desolation which the Lord knew, we need to look at some of the possible causes of what we experience as darkness and forsakenness.

Reasons for darkness

If we come to a place of dryness in our life of prayer, we can at least comfort ourselves with an Arab proverb which says, 'All sunshine makes a desert.' The darkness may be for purposes of growth. Clouds often spell rain, and rain turns barrenness into fruiting time. Like the seasons, our prayer will be rhythmic, knowing the glory of blossom but also the quiet periods of planting and secret growth when nothing *seems* to be happening. It is in the darkness of the soil that the seed germinates, in the darkness of the wardrobe that the hyacinth bulbs come on.

It is part of being human. 'Prayer goes in wavy lines',[3] says Maria Boulding. It is not a smooth straight line. It is more like a temperature chart with its ups and downs – its peaks and its troughs. And these are necessary. One of the real dangers of the spiritual life is 'plateau-ing'. As Gregory of Nyssa says, 'There will always be a great distance to run for him who is running towards the Lord. Thus he who climbs can never cease from climbing, going from fresh beginning to fresh beginning – beginnings which never have an end.'[4]

We need our ups and downs – no one can live on a 'high' all the time. We need, too, our balance of light and darkness. Too much light is unbearable. In the land of the midnight sun, some people are driven frantic for *want* of darkness. Rhythm and fluctuation in prayer need not alarm us then – a complacent, static state should.

There may have been times when we have burdened ourselves with unnecessary guilt by assuming that all darkness is the direct result of sin, whereas it is by no means always so. It certainly was not the cause of Jesus' dereliction. On the other hand, if there *is* unacknowledged sin in our lives, it will inevitably obscure our vision of God. If we have turned away from the light then we shall, of course, be walking in darkness. We shall need to re-turn, face in the right direction again and 'walk towards the shining of the light' (cf. Baruch 4:2). Life seems to be made up of so many of these turnings, these conversions, made possible through penitence and confession.

Our darkness could be connected with some crisis – at work, in the family or the church. Perhaps there are major changes ahead and the general feeling of uncertainty and bewilderment has affected us spiritually.

It could even be part of a mid-life crisis. No, that is not a joke! Mid-life has now been recognised as such a traumatic time for some that, in the USA at any rate, mid-life crisis clinics have been set up. It can be a time of great self-questioning and self-doubt. For some it is the time when they see younger people getting promotion and taking on the responsibilities they have carried or would like to have carried and now never will. Inevitably this brings a loss of self-confidence. Self-worth is challenged. All of which will affect our prayer.

Or the darkness may be due to the season of the year. The winter solstice greatly affects some. Year after year, they battle with depression through the darker months. It is sufficiently common a condition for research to have been conducted into the use of light therapy with seemingly encouraging results. We cannot equate spiritual depression with clinical depression, but there is frequently an interaction between the two. It is not appropriate here to go into technical distinctions between different forms of depression, breakdown, ministry burn-out, 'spiritual blues', the dark night of the soul or the dark night of the senses – rather to recognise that darkness and desolation in prayer could spring from one or other of these, or none. It might simply be fatigue, and a sensible reappraisal of our workload and some judicial cancellations in our diaries may be the answer.

Then, too, let us not forget that our experience of darkness could be on behalf of someone else. We carry their bewilderment and pain in the mysterious coinherence of human life. We do not know its origins, nor will we necessarily know the results of having borne it. All that is asked of us at these times is fidelity, and perhaps gratitude that God trusts us to share the load.

Darkness is sometimes the next step on after an experience of charismatic renewal. Following the wonder, the excitement, the joy of a new in-filling of the Holy Spirit, accompanied perhaps by gifts, there comes a rather different period. Not only does the excitement die down, there may actually come a feeling of distaste in worship and a reluctance to pray. The songs that we once found so moving now jar. The prayer that flowed so freely and naturally seems to have dried up completely. It can be alarming. Does it mean that the experience of renewal was phoney, simply a flash in the pan? Does the present boredom invalidate all that we thought had taken place? We become anxious. What if our friends knew how we were feeling? If only we could be open about it! Keeping up a front is so wearing.

On the contrary, if this is our experience, we should take heart. It is not necessarily a bad sign. It does not mean that the gift of the Holy Spirit was just an induced experience in the context of an exciting gathering of like-minded people. It probably means that we have moved on to the next stage – an altogether quieter, less dramatic and less obvious period in our growth, but nevertheless, deeply significant. The renewal has gone down into the bloodstream and is working through our whole being. It is a time of assimilation. Not only do we find ourselves drawn more to a contemplative silence but we shall discover another side to the work of the Holy Spirit, for part of his work is to overshadow. He overshadowed at creation to bring order out of chaos. He overshadowed the virgin Mary at the annunciation when she received the incarnate Word, and he will overshadow us 'till Christ be formed in us'. But shadows cast darkness.

In his book *A Way Through the Wilderness*, Jamie Buckingham records a telling conversation.

> One afternoon I enquired of that lovable old Dutch saint, Corrie ten Boom, about the silence and darkness of God. Years before, when she was 50 years of age, she had been forced into a Nazi Concentration Camp. There her old father and dear sister died horrible deaths. Yet out of that wilderness she learned the truth of Psalm 91: 'He that dwelleth in the secret place of the most High shall abide under the shadow of the Almighty'. (AV)
>
> She was 80 when I talked to her. 'Even though we are to walk in the light with our brothers and sisters', she told me, 'there comes a time, as you draw close to God, that you are consumed with darkness. This is true when you are abiding in the shadow. The closer you get to God, the less you understand him. In the darkness of his presence, under the shadow of the Almighty, we learn to believe.'[5]

The search for the hidden God

There are those who argue that the Song of Songs should never have been included in the canon of scripture. It is far too erotic! But we should be much the poorer without it, for it gives us one of the most vivid symbols of someone in spiritual darkness. The woman in the song rushes round frenetically looking for him whom her soul loves. But he is extraordinarily elusive, appearing at the window, knocking at the door, vanishing into the night . . . until, all caution thrown to the winds, she runs round the streets asking the watchmen if they have seen him whom her soul loves, and vowing that when she finds him she will cling to him and never let him go.

Haven't we all known times when, like that woman, we have plunged around in the darkness looking for the Lord, crying out with Isaiah, 'Truly, thou art a God who hidest thyself' (Isa 45:15), and looking for the quickest exit out of the darkness? We have failed to realise that if we could be still instead of getting into such a panic, we might discover what Isaiah calls the 'treasures of darkness' (Isa 45:3), those secrets which are only ever disclosed in the dark.

Like Mary Magdalene (and liturgically the woman in the Song of Songs is seen as a type of Mary Magdalene), we stand weeping at the tomb of all that has been real and has had meaning for us in the past, asking of the Stranger who comes: 'Have you seen him whom my soul loves? If you know where they have laid him, tell me . . .' And then there is a response. Perhaps it is our name we hear; whatever it is, it is a moment of recognition, an indefinable personal something that assures us it is the Lord. We determine to hold on to him, never to let him go from our grasp again. But he has to say to us, 'Don't cling to me' – that is, 'Don't imprison me in your preconceived expectations. Don't try to fix me in the familiar. I won't be conformed to your patterns and ideas'. The risen Christ is a free Christ and it is impossible to pin him down. 'He is the stranger in the garden, the stranger on the shore, the stranger on the road eluding identification and control.' We shall not be allowed to cling to past experiences and old images for security. 'Touch me not . . .' Perhaps there is a sense in which sometimes we *have* to lose touch. Rowan Williams has said that all of us have to lose Christ at times in order to discover him afresh in deeper resurrection power; in order to 'recover him in as drastically new a way' as when we first met and loved him.[6]

Like the disciples at the tomb, we find he is constantly 'not here', as the angels said. Elusive and unpredictable, he turns up in unexpected guises and disguises, often surprising us by joy. We recognise him by the strange burning in our hearts, a memory reawakened, a familiar presence dawning upon our consciousness as we emerge from the darkness. We, too, leap up, saying, 'It is the Lord!' (John 21:7).

The lover in the Song of Songs seemed to be having a game of hide and seek with his beloved, playing hard to get. But why should God want to do that with us in prayer? Should he not be encouraging us, rather than putting difficulties in the way?

It is to test the genuineness of our longing for God – to see if we are prepared to 'walk by faith and not by sight'. Have we learnt a right dependence on him and on others within the body of Christ, or do we have to be propped up with 'cordials' and 'consolations'?[7] If so, the Lord taps us gently on the shoulder and says, 'Time to grow up! No more sweets now.' We may then experience something akin to withdrawal symptoms as our customary props are removed and our wells run dry. But we are being trained in a deeper faith. 'Do not trouble about anything but loving him, never mind if you cannot see him,' said Francois Malaval. 'That is why God so wisely directs the work of our salvation that he takes us by the hand without letting us see the way he is leading us, save what is necessary to the capacity of each one.'[8]

The darkness sorts out whether we seek him whom our soul loves – or his gifts. Is it really God we desire, or are our desires as mixed as our motives? If so, the darkness will do a purging work. Is it really God we want, or some sensible consolation of his felt presence? Is it really God we want, or an experience of God? Is it really God we want, or deeper prayer, spiritual growth, greater freedom in the Spirit . . . all of which are very good in themselves. But they are God's gifts, not God himself. In fact, they can become a form of self-seeking.

'Lift up your heart to God with humble love: and mean himself, and not what you can get out of him,' said the author of the *Cloud of Unknowing*.[9] 'Him I covet, him I seek and nothing but him.'[10]

So it is not prayer we seek in prayer, but God himself. Not an experience of God, but 'the living God inherent in yet transcending all experience'.[11] How far have we been guilty of spiritual cupboard love – wanting God's gifts rather than God himself?

The darkness will keep us searching, like the woman in the Song, for the one we love. That is not to say that he has never found us or we him. The use of the word 'search' here means

an ever-deepening longing for God, an ever-increasing inten-
sification of desire for him which is not a restless rushing
around looking for him in this prayer group, that book or a
particular meditation technique. St Bernard speaks of it as 'a
searching never satisfied yet without any restlessness . . . that
eternal, inexplicable longing that knows no dissatisfaction or
want'.[12]

'My beloved is mine and I am his' said the woman in the
Song, and St Augustine, especially towards the end of his life,
reduces the springs of Christian living almost exclusively to
the 'blind pulling of desire'. It will keep us straining forward
eagerly – a favourite expression of Gregory of Nyssa. The
same verb is used by Paul when he speaks of 'forgetting what
lies behind and straining forward to what lies ahead, I press on
toward the goal for the prize of the upward call of God in
Christ Jesus' (Phil 3:13,14). Straining forward like an athlete
eager to be first to breast the tape, like a dog happy to be
taken for a walk but longing to be off the lead and racing
ahead. The 'straining forward', the yearning, may still be
going on in the depths of the will, even though the surface
levels of our being are numb with weariness, disillusionment,
pain and, yes, even boredom! The church fathers used to call
this state, *Accidie*. Take heart – the saints were all familiar
with it too! At such times it is not our desire that is being
tested but our fidelity.

If our longings for God were met with instant satisfaction
(as most things are in these days of instant everything) then
our desire would not intensify. Contrary to other areas of life
where the continual *satisfaction* of desires leads to addictive
and compulsive tendencies, it is the seeming *withholding of
satisfaction* that increases and deepens our desire for God. As
Gregory of Nyssa puts it, 'The reward of the search is to go on
searching. The soul's desire is fulfilled by the very fact of it
remaining unsatisfied, for really to see God is never to have
had one's fill of desiring him.'[13]

Dazzling darkness

We owe a great debt to Gregory of Nyssa, for he, along with Pseudo-Dionysius the Areopagite, was the greatest exponent of the apophatic tradition,[14] which taught that the darkness is only seeming darkness. In fact, it is really the light of God. Dazzling darkness, they called it. So bright is the light of God, it causes temporary blindness, just as when we have stared into the sun for a while, everything around seems black. Or to change the image, like bats we can be blinded by the light. Our darkness then is due not to an absence of light but an excess of it. 'Absence symbolises ignorance, excess symbolises a transcendent unknowing.'[15]

This, of course, is a very different darkness from that experienced by Jesus on the cross. There he entered into the darkness of God's judgment on sin. It was not *seeming* darkness. It *was* darkness. Only from the other side of the cross, and with the eyes of faith, can we see the rays of glory that shone out from that dreadful darkness. When sometimes God trusts his loved ones to enter into the darkness of his judgment – perhaps for the sin of a nation or a community then, as for Jesus, the experience of sorrow and pain is so intense that they are not able to *feel* the glory or the atoning power that works through the darkness.

Sometimes it is only in the dark that we can travel. This can be physically true, but also spiritually true. At such times we can regard the darkness as 'the friendly night' – the title given to a chapter in Carlo Carretto's *Letters from the Desert*.[16] He tells how during the day the sun made it impossible to 'navigate' through the desert wastes, but at night the stars provided numerous points of reference to prevent the travellers getting lost.

Darkness is, therefore, sometimes related to vision. It seems that the blessings of God are often preceded or followed by darkness. John Bunyan discovered this:

Though God doth visit my soul with never so blessed a discovery of himself, yet I have found again, that such

hours have attended me afterwards that I have been in my
spirit so filled with darkness, that I could not so much as
once conceive what that God and comfort was, with which I
have been refreshed.[17]

Perhaps we should remind ourselves of the need for holy
fear when we ask for spiritual vision. For 'vision is an extor-
tionate trafficker. Not content with demanding a price in
advance, she exacts almost as heavy a price at the end. A
moment of insight has to be paid for by months – years maybe
– of spiritual aridity.'[18]

The spiritual writings of every age and tradition speak of
this experience. 'Before God doth dispense great revelations
and comforts, he doth sometimes desert.'[19]

If we *know* that moments of illumination will be surrounded by darkness, that 'a glimpse of celestial light' will
make 'the shadows of earth more oppressive',[20] then we shall
not be tempted to give up when the going gets hard. It is never
easy in the darkness to believe that there is light ahead: in the
midst of his sufferings on the cross it is unlikely that Jesus was
consoled by thoughts of resurrection.

Many souls have undertaken, and daily do undertake, this
way, and they persevere while they keep the sweet relish of
their primitive fervour; yet this sweetness and sensible
delight is scarce done, but presently, when they are overtaken by storms of trouble, temptation and aridity . . . they
falter and turn back: a clear sign that they sought themselves, and not God.[21]

Sometimes when God wants to make it quite clear that it is
he who is at work in our soul, that the growth is entirely due to
him and nothing to do with human achievement, he calls upon
the service of his handmaid, darkness. It enables him to work
unhindered as an anaesthetic allows a surgeon to operate
freely.

'My dry root would take more dew and summer's-rain than

it getteth, were it not that Christ will have dryness and deadness in us to work upon.'[22]

In the dark, but not alone

Whatever the reason the Lord asks us to suffer darkness in the spiritual life, and however much we may experience it as loss – loss of joy, loss of certainty, loss of inclination, and, above all, loss of *him* – we can be certain, with Teresa of Avila, that he has not left us to face it alone.

The story is told of a Native American boy preparing for his initiation ceremony. He had to undergo a series of tests, the last and most dreadful of which was to spend a night in the forest – alone. On the appointed night his father took the boy into the forest, collected an ample supply of wood and lit a fire. Giving him strict instructions to keep the fire going all night, he left, promising to return first thing in the morning. All night the lad shivered and sweated alternately, in sheer terror. Every sound of a snapping twig or beating of wings convinced him a wild animal was approaching. And, as if that were not sufficient to contend with, the forest was full of evil spirits to haunt and frighten a young boy.

The night seemed interminable, but gradually the blackness gave place to the grey of dawn and he began to distinguish the trunks of the trees. As the light grew stronger he became aware of a tall shape that was not, as he had at first imagined, a tree trunk, but the figure of a man standing motionless beside a tree. It was his father. He had been there all the time.[23]

Paul tells us that, 'In Christ God was reconciling the world to himself' (2 Cor 5:19). He did not abandon his Son to suffer alone, even though Jesus' sense of separation and dereliction was absolutely genuine. How else would that terrible cry have been wrung from him on the cross?

What we do know, and can take comfort from, is that the passion was a shared passion and that even in that terrible darkness God was 'there all the time', agonising with his Son.

No less, when he calls us to share in the ongoing passion of Christ, completing what is lacking in his afflictions (Col 1:24), he will be there all the time, despite the fact that we have no feeling of his presence – indeed, only an appalling darkness like that of a forest at night.

It was to those who, under persecution, were likely to be sharing in Christ's sufferings very literally, that Peter wrote words that have been a source of comfort to Christians down through the ages, whatever the form of their trial and testing:

Beloved, do not be surprised at the fiery ordeal which comes upon you to prove you, as though something strange were happening to you. But rejoice in so far as you share Christ's sufferings, that you may also rejoice and be glad when his glory is revealed . . . And after you have suffered a little while, the God of all grace, who has called you to his eternal glory in Christ, will himself restore, establish, and strengthen you.

(1 Pet 4:12,13; 5:10)

10

'INTO YOUR HANDS' – the prayer of commitment

Then Jesus, crying with a loud voice, said, 'Father, into thy
hands I commit my spirit!'

(Luke 23:46)

'My God, why hast thou forsaken me?' began as an expression of the desolation felt by the people of Israel. It was taken
up and used very personally by Jesus in his moment of
greatest dereliction, and it has been echoed by Christians
down through the years ever since, as they have entered into
something of the experience of God's seeming absence. Yet,
because in the darkness God is there all the time, it becomes a
growing point, a time of transformation, a participation in
Christ's victory through seeming failure. Paradox lies deep at
the heart of the Christian life!

When Jesus spoke these words on the cross, total aloneness
and full acceptance touched each other. In that moment of
complete emptiness all was fulfilled. In that hour of darkness new light was seen. While death was witnessed, life
was affirmed. Where God's absence was most loudly
expressed, his presence was most profoundly revealed.[1]

The prayer of abandonment to God

'My God, why hast thou forsaken me?' answers itself in the
prayer that followed, 'Father, into thy hands I commit my

spirit.' After that, 'he dismissed his spirit' (Matt 27:50 Living Bible). The prayer of desolation is not prayed in isolation from the prayer of commitment, of total trust in the Father. And what the Master did, should not his disciples do also? How often when we feel abandoned do *we* then abandon ourselves to God's mercy praying, 'Into your hands, Lord, I commit . . . everything'?

Just as Jesus used the words of a psalm to express his forsakenness, so now he turns to the psalms to express his commitment (Ps 31:5). In his desolation he began his prayer with 'My God'. In trust, the 'My God' gives way to 'Father'.

'Into thy hands . . .' brings us a sense of a serene handing over of his soul.

We deepen our isolation from the prayer by talking non-sense about it. Jesus, we say, had the power to dismiss his spirit; we do not. Therefore the prayer is special to Jesus and bears no relationshp to our own lives. It is for Good Friday, sad faces and solemn music.[2]

We do have evidence, however, that people in the Third World can often tell when they are dying – even to the day and the hour. In the West we have still retained something of that intuition. The patient dying of cancer very often knows it in the depth of his being, without or before being told.

Certainly the patriarchs all knew when they were dying. Therefore the prayer of Jesus must not be regarded as something peculiar to his redemptive work. He was showing us how to die. He was dying in the proper manner, dying the death of a believer, praying the final prayer as it ought to be prayed.[3]

Had this perhaps been one of the prayers he would have prayed regularly every night in the third hour of prayer? And now, in an hour of extremity, it springs to his lips very naturally?

In the Office of Compline, the last Office of the day for

those of us in Religious Communities, these words are
repeated every night:

> Into your hands, I commit my spirit:
> You will redeem me, O Lord God of truth.

As we go into the dark of the night, so we say, 'Into your
hands, Lord.' For every time we lie down to sleep, it is a little
death. What better prayer to pray, then? It is not, of course,
prayed for ourselves alone, but for all who face darkness of
whatever sort, that their desolation might be matched with
trustful commitment.

Jesus was 'handed over' to his enemies by Judas, 'handed
over' by the scribes and elders to Pilate, 'handed over' by
Pilate first to the multitude and then to the soldiers to be
scourged. Finally he was 'handed over' to be crucified.

Now *he* is free to do the 'handing over', and in complete
trust he commits himself into the hands of his Father. The
words of another psalm are appropriate: 'I have calmed and
quieted my soul like a weaned child upon its mother's breast:
like a child on its mother's breast is my soul within me. O
Israel, trust in the Lord' (Ps 131:2, 3 NTW) – just like that . . .
like a child. One of the most endearing things about children
is their trustfulness.

Trusting the one who knows and loves

In putting himself into the hands of God, Jesus is not simply
entrusting his life, but his work too. He commits his whole
mission, 'the work which thou gavest me to do' (John 17:4).
He is able to cry, 'It is finished' and leave it, and the whole
future, to the Father. The great chorus, 'Achievèd is the
glorious work' in Haydn's oratorio, *Creation*, could aptly be
sung to celebrate this achievement of the passion. He had
done what he came to do and now he lets go. It is all handed
over to God.

That is a lesson most of us find hard to learn. Somehow, we

cannot let go of a particular job or role. We do what we can, and then, instead of leaving it at that, we continue to worry and look back over our shoulders at the might-have-beens. So much of our life seems to entail learning how to hand everything over to God, to give him back what is his by rights. We continue to carry burdens unnecessarily, we plan out our lives instead of letting him reveal *his* plans, we stupidly try to conceal the sins he longs to receive and heal, handling the failures he would gladly deal with, and we feed our egos on the praise which belongs to him. Even when we try to hand over all the glory, it is so easy to scoop up a little on the side for ourselves.

'Father, into thy hands . . .' These words are the climax of a total submission through suffering – the *'sacrament of nothing withheld'*.[4] We can take them as our own and use them as

a way of total self-abandonment to God without understanding, content to be united to him in the dark if needs be, willing to accept the mystery of self and of life and death once and for all, in order to trust and leave it finally and peacefully with him . . .[5]

We become very vulnerable when we trust ourselves completely to another – whether it be to the hands of a surgeon as we submit to an anaesthetic and all the unknown of an operation or to the skills of a pilot as we settle back in our seats for a night flight quite unable to see where we are going, and at such speed too!, or whether it is the givenness of one's self, body and soul, within marriage – it is all a great risk. But we take the risks in the one instance because we trust the expertise of the surgeon or the pilot, in the other, because trust is born of love.

In the prayer, 'Into your hands, Lord, I commit my spirit' we combine both these kinds of trust. We are submitting to the one who knows, and knows fully, and to the one who loves, and loves completely.

During World War II, a young soldier named Ian Mac-Horton fell into the hands of the Japanese in Burma and became a prisoner of war. Emaciated, very seriously wounded, entirely cut off from all contact with his fellow British soldiers and desperately weak, it seemed impossible that he could live. Certainly he posed no threat to his guards, for even if he had been able to muster the energy to escape, they were surrounded by dense jungle – the home of carnivorous animals and deadly snakes. But he was inspired by the words of Minnie Louise Haskins (made so memorable by King George VI) which his mother had sent him in a Christmas letter:

> I said to the man who stood at the gate of the year; 'Give me a light that I may tread safely into the unknown'. And he replied 'Go out into the darkness, and put your hand into the hand of God. That shall be to you better than a light and safer than a known way'.[6]

Against all odds, escape he did. He dragged himself along a path for a few days and then, too ill to go on, lay down to die. Suddenly he felt something move beside him. It was a large lizard. Slowly his mind registered that here was food and he raised his knife – but before he could strike, the lizard darted away, stumbled in a rut but picked itself up and disappeared. MacHorton forgot the lizard for his eyes were rivetted on the rut. He crawled over to examine it. It was a bootmark! A regulation British army boot with thirteen studs. Gazing in wonder, he felt the imprint and, yes, it was fairly fresh. He looked on, and there stretching ahead as far as he could see were more bootmarks. Suddenly, hope sprang up. He was jubilant as he dragged himself along the path following the footmarks. For days he followed them up hill, down dale, skirting round a treacherous swamp in complete safety. As he stopped to rest one day, he looked back over the path he had followed and his scalp began to crawl, the hairs on the back of his neck to prickle. There were no bootmarks. He crawled back a few yards and, sure enough, there were the imprints of his own naked feet – but no bootmarks at all. Panic stricken, he looked ahead – and there they were, the bootmarks stretching on as far as the eye could see. Utterly dumbfounded by the mystery of it all, he could only but follow. He began to build up a relationship with the footprints – talk to them, laugh with them, share his hopes and fears with them.

One day they stopped abruptly. He felt devastated and let down. He was hopelessly lost, stuck in the middle of nowhere without chart or compass. He had simply followed those footmarks in complete trust. Then he heard the sound of water close by, and parting the tall grass to one side of him, he saw that he had come to a river – a very wide river. He knew enough geography of the area to realise that there was only one river of that size in that part of the world, and that the British base of Tamu was only a relatively short distance up-stream.[7]

> O let me see thy footmarks,
>   And in them plant mine own;
> My hope to follow duly
>   Is in thy strength alone;
> O guide me, call me, draw me,
>   Uphold me to the end;
> And then in heaven receive me,
>   My Saviour and my Friend.[8]

'Go out into the darkness, and put your hand into the hand of God . . .'

'Into your hands, Lord, I commit my spirit.'

11

'PRAY THEN LIKE THIS . . .' – praying as Jesus taught

Pray then like this: Our Father . . .

(Matt 6:9)

So far we have been looking at the teaching of Jesus on prayer from the point of view of his precept and example. We have sought to enter imaginatively and reverently into his use of silence and need of solitude, his grounding in the scriptures and fidelity to the liturgical prayers of the Jewish people, his prayer through the senses and his contemplative wonder, his intimacy with God which he invites us to share and his intercessory love, his prayer in suffering – the agony of 'Thy will be done' and 'Why hast thou forsaken me?', his legitimate questioning of his Father and his absolute trust in him.

Outwardly, he chose special places and times to intensify and manifest his prayer: in the temple, on the mountain, in the wilderness, away from the crowd, or simply some odd spot during the day or along the road. By day and by night, alone or with his disciples, he was always praying.[1]

Praying Jesus' way

This 'man of prayer' challenges our mediocrity and half-heartedness at every level. He teaches us how to make the whole of life a prayer, and prayer the whole of life. We see his relationship with the Father and his delight in his will as his 'prayer without ceasing' (1 Thess 5:16 AV). We see his continual standing in the divine presence as man's representative to God and God's representative to man as his high priestly prayer. By identifying fully with men, experiencing life as they experience it, being tempted in every respect as we are 'yet without sin' (Heb 4:15), showing the mercy which gets inside the skin of another and sees and feels and suffers as the other (cf. Matt 5:7), he 'stood in the breach' (Ps 106:23) to bridge the chasm between sin and holiness and to open up a way of access to the Father. He became the road by which the prodigal could return home, for 'no one comes to the Father, but by me' (John 14:6). We speak of John 17 as his great high priestly prayer but, in fact, his whole life was just that. No wonder the writer to the Hebrews exhorts those 'holy brethren' who 'share in a heavenly call' to 'consider Jesus, the apostle and high priest of our confession' (Heb 3:1).

The purpose of this book has been to consider Jesus, the man of prayer. But now our final consideration in this study must be of some of the specific points that he made in his teaching. We need to lay hold of the timeless truths he left to help us in our pilgrimage.

Obviously, if we want to know how, why or where to pray, we must fix our eyes on Jesus and do as he did, because only he can teach us how to pray, through the Holy Spirit who is the supreme Spiritual Director for each of us. All of us will know times when our prayer is inexpressible. It is only capable then of articulation through the groanings of the Spirit within us (Rom 8:26). We should welcome such times, for we need to be reminded continually that it is the Holy Spirit who prays in and through us in ways that are far beyond our understanding. Our call is to be open to him, available to him through fidelity and purity of heart, and to fulfil the prerequisites for his prayer in us.

Praying persistently

The first prerequisite is *perseverance*. We are to pray as those who are importunate. What are we to make of that strange parable of the widow (Luke 18:1–8)? Are we to understand that through prayer it is within our power to change the mind of a reluctant God by much badgering? Are we to pester him until – through sheer weariness – he gives way to us, in the fashion of some indulgent human fathers?

It is not badgering that God honours but perseverance. The first has all the feel of 'getting one's own way' about it, of whining and wheedling in the way of small children. The second implies an earnestness in prayer, a steady pursuit of God that acknowledges our constant state of helplessness and our need for total dependence on him who has the power to change things. We are unlikely to continue day after day asking for those things which do not really matter to us.

We are only importunate about what is important. The extent of our perseverance indicates the depth of our desire. It means that a sifting process has already taken place and we have left behind lesser and more trivial matters and concentrated our petitionary energy on only those things that are our deepest concern. So behind this persevering, assiduous prayer there must lie a sense of urgent need, a quickened compassion, a desperate longing, a righteous anger, a sensitive conscience, etc. There is a compulsion about this prayer. The Holy Spirit has touched our hearts and laid a burden upon them. He asks us to accept the responsibility for carrying that burden to God faithfully, of *becoming* prayer for others, of continuing in prayer even when we cannot see the point for there are no apparent results. It is not always vouchsafed to us to see successes, the victories won, the walls that crumble, the triumphant shout of 'I believe' (see p. 108).

We are not cajoling God into changing his mind but responding to the invitation which in his astonishing divine self-limitation he makes, asking us to cooperate with him by acting as channels of his power, his healing, his love and his grace. Channels can be open or closed, clear or blocked. The power is there and unlimited, but because he has ordained it this way, he depends on our vigilance in prayer to help direct it to those in need.

This is no work for the fainthearted. It takes courage to persevere. 'In due season we shall reap, if we do not lose heart' (Gal 6:9). The very parable itself is introduced with the words, 'And he told them a parable, to the effect that they ought always to pray and not lose heart' (Luke 18:1).

This perseverance, however, may well be very costly. As Amy Carmichael once said,

> There is nothing ever lightly won where the deep things of the Spirit are concerned. I can remember a whole day spent pressing through the thick, thick veils of time and sense and self before at last there was a break . . .
>
> I know that at any time we may be tested by disappointment and need to ask God to give us persistence. And he will not refuse. He understands. He has told us he does. And in the end – oh joy of all joys – we shall hear the voice we love best in all the world saying to us, even to us, 'I know . . . how thou hast not fainted' (Rev 2:3)[2]

There are many who will testify to even longer periods of darkness and seeming disappointment than the one day that Amy Carmichael recalls. So the second prerequisite is *faith*. Persevering prayer will be hard, indeed impossible, unless we have faith to believe that God is using it for his own purposes and will 'accomplish that which he pleases' through it. 'Therefore I tell you, whatever you ask in prayer, believe that you have received it, and it will be yours' (Mark 11:24).

'But', some may ask, 'surely God knows what we need before we ask him? So, why ask him?' Yet the teaching of Jesus is clear. We are to ask and ask believing that whatever we ask in his name, it will be granted (Matt 7:7; 17:20,21). 'And whatever you ask in prayer, you will receive, if you have faith' (Matt 21:22). A father knows what his child needs, but it still delights his heart when the child asks for it. It is saying something important about their relationship.

In *The Pilgrim's Progress*, the Reliever, who had greatly helped the women pilgrims in their troubles and dangers, said, 'I marvelled much . . . that you petitioned not the Lord for a conductor.' And Christiana replied, 'But since our Lord knew it would be for our profit, I wonder that he sent not one along with us!'

The Reliever answered, 'It is not always necessary to grant things not asked for . . . and "tis a poor thing not worth asking for".'[3]

The asking should, then, be trusting and also sincere. Praying is not to be a matter of outward formulae; not the multiple repetition of pious phrases that neither mirror nor bear any relation to the inner disposition of the heart. 'This people honours me with their lips, but their heart is far from me . . .' (Matt 15:8). Nor is there any value in wordiness in prayer that masks emptiness. 'And in praying do not heap up empty phrases as the Gentiles do; for they think that they will be heard for their many words' (Matt 6:7). 'Pray temperately and simply. Prayer needs no brilliant ideas, no flood of words. Gradually you should come to pure and simple listening to the one who has the words of eternal life' (John 6:68).[4] Only sincere prayer will lift off and take wing.

The words of Ecclesiasticus 43:27 come to mind here: 'Though we speak much we cannot reach the end: and the sum of our words is – He is the all.' (Version used in *The Daily Office* of the Community of St Mary the Virgin and the Community of St Peter Woring. Part 1. page 7. – a private publication for Community use only, in which 'Scriptural texts are a combination of several different translations' cf. Acknowledgments p. iv.)

Yes, and his Spirit too – for his compassion matches 'indeed inspires' our yearning – is ever taking our human frailty by the hand. *We* are not even sure what boons should rightly be the object of our prayers; but his Spirit – his very Spirit – is pleading ever for us with sighings such as no language can shape into words. Ah, but he who tracks the labyrinth of the heart needs no words to divine what the Spirit means: he knows that his Spirit intercedes for his hallowed ones *in just the way that God desires.*[5]

(Rom 8:26, 27 The Living Bible).

Praying sincerely

Jesus also taught that the offering of prayer could not be made sincerely while there were unresolved grievances and quarrels lurking around. The offering should be left in abeyance until reconciliation has been made (Matt 5:24). Are we then to stop praying after a row with someone, until we have made it up? Certainly the last thing we often *feel* like doing is praying as we fume and lick our wounds. The anger that springs from personal hurt can certainly be destructive of the prayer that opens channels for God's reconciling love to reach others. But Jesus clearly regarded the nursing of grudges, the fanning of smouldering anger till it burns into renewed flame, as far worse and more damaging to relationships in the long run and, therefore, to prayer than the explosive outburst that wounds but is quickly over and healed. Both are regrettable, but none of us is likely to get through life without at some time meting out anger or being on its receiving end. We can, however, bring such disputes and storms to a close by a forgiving spirit on the one hand and humility on the other. It is the unwillingness or even refusal to forgive that Jesus so roundly condemns: it makes nonsense of prayer and invalidates even the observance of the externals and rituals of worship (Matt 5:21–24).

For prayer to be a sincere offering, the attitude of the heart must be right even if there hasn't been an opportunity to bring about reconciliation. And the right attitude is one which has an overall intention to forgive and be forgiven, not to perpetuate a rift or allow a wound to fester till it is a stinking sore. It is the attitude of the peacemaker, and such people are both brave and big-hearted. As David Watson discovered, reconciliation matters more to God than a 'successful' ministry:

> About one a.m. on Advent Sunday morning, I had a bad asthmatic attack. In my helplessness I cried out to God to speak to me. I'm not very good at listening to God, but between one and three a.m. God spoke to me so powerfully and painfully that I have never felt so broken before him (and still do). He showed me that all my preaching, writing and other ministry was absolutely *nothing* compared to my love relationship with him. In fact, my sheer busyness had squeezed out the close intimacy I had known with him during the first few months of the year after my operation. God also showed me that any 'love' for him meant *nothing* unless I was truly able to love from my heart my brother or sister in Christ. As the Lord put various names into my mind, I began to write letters to about twelve people asking for forgiveness for hurting them, for still being inwardly angry against them – or whatever. It was the most painful pruning and purging I can remember in my entire Christian life. But fruitful! Already some replies to my letters have reduced me to tears.[6]

For all sorts of reasons, reconciliation may not be possible or even advisable *immediately*. Nor must we imagine that it is necessarily right to force a premature apology or request for forgiveness. Anxiety and an inability to stay with pain leave us restless until we have sorted things out with the offending or injured party. We are concerned not to 'let the sun go down on our anger', so we do not allow the essential space needed to stand back, distance ourselves from the situation, get it into perspective and indeed trace the pain to its real source.

At times we are all deeply wounded by a breakdown in a relationship. The wounds are out of all proportion to the immediate event. We then need time to sink below the level of the surface pain of the actual quarrel, to reach down to those memories in the depths of our being which are related to it but not caused by it. This kind of pain sets in motion a whole chain reaction that triggers off a host of unhealed memories from the past that are all contributing to the present situation and feeding it with all sorts of messages.

By biding the right moment, the apology can be given and received appropriately and at a deep level; the *real* problem exposed, perhaps. The healing can then be lasting. But hasty apologies given because it is 'the right thing to do', will sometimes close the door to a fuller exploration of the roots and origins of our problems in relationship, and prevent fuller healing and growth.

Blessed indeed are the peacemakers, which is very different from being a peace-lover who cannot bear rows and therefore refuses to face the pain of creative conflict.

On two other occasions Jesus touched on the priority of sincerity in prayer. First, when he advocated secrecy in prayer (Matt 6:5,6). Never is prayer to be put on for 'show', never should it be paraded to win the acclaim of men. It may well do that – but that will be its only result; nothing more. God will not be impressed, nor can he use such prayer as a channel of his power to others. In fact, it isn't prayer – it is hypocrisy, which, in its literal sense, is play-acting. The actors may enjoy themselves, but they are not in touch with God who is reality.

Second, in the parable of the two men who went to the temple to pray (Luke 18:9–14) – the one a Pharisee and the other a tax collector – Jesus illustrated the need for humility as an essential element in prayer. Pride, self-justification, boosting the ego by dwelling on the unworthiness of others, reciting one's goodnesses, glorying in the illusion of self-sufficiency and harbouring inflated ideas of one's own importance have no part in true prayer. As Jesus made clear, the tax collector whose sense of utter need made him cry out, who recognised his sinful nature and exposed it to God's steadfast love and mercy, had got to the heart of prayer despite his dubious professional life. He came in humility – in sincerity and truth. His was the prayer of poverty, and 'a prayer out of a poor man's mouth reacheth to the ears of God' (Ecclus 21:5 AV).

Praying together

'Where two or three are gathered in my name,' said Jesus, 'there am I in the midst of them' (Matt 18:20). He also said 'If two of you agree on earth about anything they ask, it will be done for them by my Father in heaven' (Matt 18:19).

There is no explanation given as to why special authority is given to a small group praying together. He merely advocated something that he himself had practised, for clearly he valued cooperation in the work of prayer. There were those special occasions when he asked certain disciples to be 'with him' – particularly Peter, James and John. They were the ones who were with him when he raised Jairus' daughter from the dead. He asked the same three to accompany him to the mountain where he prayed and became transfigured. And again he sought their support as he prayed in the garden of Gethsemane . . . only they fell asleep.

If in prayer each of us becomes a channel for God to reach others, it means that in a group of people the channel widens for the inflow and outflow of his love.

We have to be careful not to be simplistic and reduce God's ability to act to a question of mathematics. If we follow this line of thought too literally, we shall for ever be trying to organise mass prayer meetings on the assumption that they will bring mass results. Yet there *is* a place for a nationwide call to prayer and fasting. The focusing of prayer on a particular need by a large number of people increases the seriousness and quality of each individual prayer. The well-known example of the single coal which quickly dies on its own but is kindled and glows when united to other coals to create a mighty blaze, applies here. And the sum total of that is effective. We are the body of Christ and we need to know that, in prayer, we are linked with other members of the body in united concern and petition. Whether or not we are together physically, we are of course linked together every time we pray.

> Before thy throne we daily meet
> As joint-petitioners to thee;
> In spirit we each other greet . . .[7]

said Richard Baxter, and though he spoke of those parted from us by death, it could equally apply to those separated by distance.

Although we know that even when we pray alone there is no such thing as *private* prayer when we belong to the body of Christ, we need those times when we express our corporateness literally by gathering to pray together, we need the sense of support it gives, the increased energy of desire and the mutual comforting – strengthening. We grow disheartened when we always 'go it alone'.

So we see that in his teaching on prayer Jesus spoke of and practised prayer alone *and* together. He regularly sought the solitude essential to spiritual growth and deep intimacy with the Father. But he also knew the need for the support of two or three, and from the gospels it seems it was always at a specific and crucial point in his ministry.

'OUR FATHER IN HEAVEN' – the prayer given specifically to disciples

Our Father

The specific teaching which Jesus gave in response to the disciples' request, 'Lord, teach us to pray', (Luke 11:1) was, of course, the Lord's Prayer – a comprehensive, all-embracing prayer. Is there anything to our spiritual or material wellbeing that is omitted from it?

Our intimate relationship with our Father is renewed as we begin the prayer. His power is claimed and released upon the world by the hallowing of his name. The kingdom of God which Jesus inaugurated on earth is hastened a little more towards its fulfilment as we pray for it to be established here and now in our hearts and the hearts of all men, changing society by its reversal of worldly standards and conforming it to the law of love. We acknowledge that this can only happen through obedience to the divine will and we unite ourselves to Jesus' glad acceptance of it in, 'Thy will be done.' We are reminded that we live provisionally, i.e. as those who are provided for by a Father who knows how to give good gifts to his children, understanding their need even before they ask; who sustains us with food for the body and food for the soul; who asks that, as members of his kingdom, we should learn the secret of companionship (Latin: *companionem* [*panis* = bread] – with bread) and share our 'bread' – material or spiritual – in fellowship with one another (Acts 2:44–47; 1 Cor 11:20,29). We receive healing of body, mind and spirit through forgiveness, and are challenged as we recall that some of our ills (both physical and spiritual) stem from unconfessed sin. But like the debtor who was forgiven so much, by receiving full pardon and forgiveness we ourselves are, *ipso facto*, bound to show a forgiving spirit to those who have wronged us. Finally, we affirm our faith that, in all the situations of life, God can and will deliver us from evil.

Although the Lord's Prayer is comprehensive, covering the essential areas of our life, and can be prayed in all manner of situations, it was not meant to be used universally and indiscriminately. It was initially given to the disciples as the specific and distinctive possession of that particular group, in the same way that other rabbis taught a special prayer to their followers and their followers alone.

As, after Pentecost, more and more people were added daily to the church, so the apostles taught the prayer to all who became followers of 'the Way'. With the development of ecclesiastical structures and traditions and the threat of persecution, it became customary for the prayer to be taught to catechumens on the eve of their baptism. It was not a prayer to be said lightly or to be bandied around by all and sundry – including pagans.

That truth still holds today. Practically everybody *knows* the Lord's Prayer – it is taught in school from an early age. But few are able to pray it with meaning.

To this day I suckle at the Lord's Prayer like a child, and as an old man eat and drink from it and never get my fill. It is the very best prayer, even better than the psalter, which is so very dear to me. It is surely evident that a real master composed and taught it. What a great pity that the prayer of such a master is prattled and chattered so irreverently all over the world! How many pray the Lord's Prayer several thousand times in the course of a year, and if they were to keep on doing so for a thousand years they would not have tasted nor prayed one iota, one dot, of it! In a word, the Lord's Prayer is the greatest martyr on earth (as are the name and word of God). Everybody tortures and abuses it; few take comfort and joy in its proper use . . .'[1]

In his book *Living the Lord's Prayer*, Carroll Simcox makes a similar observation.

> We often hear it said that the Lord's Prayer is one prayer which everybody can offer. This is an amiable statement, but a complete fallacy. The only persons who can *pray* it, as distinguished from merely *saying* it, are extraordinarily devout Christians who deeply fear and love God. It is the most spiritually demanding of all prayers. Jesus did not teach it to everybody and he did not commend it to everybody.[2]

It is important to notice that the invitation to address God in the intimacy of Abba uses the first person plural pronoun, 'our'. No matter where the Christian prays this prayer, he does so in solidarity with other believers, whether he literally joins them, say in a crowded cathedral, or joins them in spirit within the privacy of his bedroom. When prayer tends to become too individualistic and subjective, we need to be reminded that Jesus gave this prayer as a corporate gift to his followers to be prayed in unity within the family of God.

> Thou callest him 'Father' as a son; but do not claim anything specifically for thyself. He is the Father of Christ alone specially, he is Father of us all in common, because he begot him alone, us he created. Therefore say thou also through grace, 'Our Father,' that thou mayest deserve to be a son.[3]

Hallowed be your name

Christians in the early church would hardly need to ask *why* they should hallow the divine name. They knew that to hallow a name was to revere the person contained in that name.

To hallow the sacred name would be to stand in awe and reverence before God. Furthermore, there was power in that name – power to be claimed! David did so quite literally when he faced Goliath:

> You come to me with a sword and with a spear and with a javelin; but I come to you *in the name of the Lord of hosts* . . . This day the Lord deliver you into my hand, and I will strike you down . . . that all the earth may know that there is a God in Israel . . .'
>
> (1 Sam 17:45,46)

Jewish Christians would have been familiar with the prophecy of Isaiah with its great acclamations of faith in the name rolling one upon another like great waves: 'O Lord, thou art my God; I will exalt thee, I will praise thy name; for thou hast done wonderful things' (Isa 25:1). 'O Lord our God, other lords besides thee have ruled over us, but thy name alone we acknowledge' (Isa 26:13). 'In the path of thy judgments, O Lord, we wait for thee; thy memorial name is the desire of our soul' (Isa 26:8). That divine power was now theirs to claim *in the name of Jesus* (Mark 9:38–41; 16:17).

Not only had Jesus specifically said, 'If you ask anything of the Father, he will give it to you in my name' (John 16:23) and told them that devils would be cast out and men healed in his name, it had been proved true in the first post-Pentecostal miracle when, in the name of Jesus, the man lame for over forty years was commanded to get up and walk – and he did (Acts 3:1–10). The rulers of the temple and Sadducees were distinctly nervous at such an occurrence and forbad the apostles to speak or preach in the name any more. But it was rather like Canute trying to drive back the sea. The power of the name had already been seen to be amazingly efficacious and there could be no withholding it now. For as Peter said: 'there is salvation in no one else, for there is no other name under heaven given among men by which we must be saved' (Acts 4:12), and it will ultimately be 'at the Name of Jesus' that every knee will bow (Phil 2:10). This will be the new and secret name written on the white stone which will be given to us in eternity (Rev 2:17). This is the name before which devils will always tremble and flee. 'Flog your enemies with the Name of Jesus,' urged St John Climacus, 'for there is no weapon more powerful in heaven or on earth.'[4]

The name is power but it is not a magic talisman. It can only be invoked with faith, love and trust in the One whose whole being is embraced in it. It should be spoken with holy awe. We cannot take it lightly on our lips without destroying some of the reverence we should have for him in our hearts. We cannot dishonour his name without dishonouring him and encouraging others to do so. For this reason it became, and still is, the practice of some Christians to bow the head a little at every mention of the name of Jesus. The very way some people speak that name reveals their great reverence for and deep relationship with the Lord. It is almost as though, momentarily, a window has been opened on to their soul.

Bruce Marshall has captured this truth in his endearing, but fictitious, character, Father Malachy – the figure at the centre of his novels.

Now when Father Malachy pronounced the Sacred Name he did not, like many priests, articulate it as though it were 'Ramsay MacDonald'; but he spoke it slowly and reverently so that the syllables seemed to be printed before the eyes in scarlet and gold, as indeed they are in illuminated mediaeval missals. And Canon Geoghegan and the Reverend Humphrey Hamilton hearing him, knew, each in his own way, that here was a man to whom the practice of religion was as important as the theory.[5]

No wonder the *Book of Common Prayer's* collect for the Second Sunday after Trinity prays, 'make us to have a perpetual fear and love of thy holy Name'.

Each time the divine name is hallowed, the way is opened for the redemption of a little more of the world. Paul tells us that the whole of 'creation waits with eager longing . . . [to] be set free from its bondage to decay' (Rom 8:19,21). Each reverent invocation of the name of Jesus is a step towards final freedom. Each mention of it is like a light shining into the universe.

Those who call upon the name by praying the Jesus Prayer know that it is

> not escapist and world-denying but, on the contrary, intensely affirmative. It does not imply a rejection of God's creation, but the reassertion of the ultimate value of everything and everyone in God. As Dr Nadejda Gorodetzky says: 'We can apply this Name to people, books, flowers, to all things we meet, see or think. The Name of Jesus may become a mystical key to the world, an instrument of the hidden offering of everything and everyone, setting the divine seal on the world. One might perhaps speak here of the priesthood of all believers. In union with our High Priest, we implore the Spirit: Make my prayer into a sacrament.'[6]

'Hallowed be your name' is of crucial importance to, and inextricably linked with, the next petition in the prayer – 'Your kingdom come'. This is a kingdom prayer and, as we have seen, the kingdom will be 'hastened' by the hallowing of the name and all that it implies.

Your kingdom come

To pray, '*Your kingdom come*' is to further yet more the process of the final transformation of all things – that redemption of which Paul speaks (Roms 8:12–28).

'The kingdom of God has come upon you', said Jesus (Matt 12:28), but it had not fully done so. The kingdom is *now* but also *not yet*. It will not finally be established on earth until the transformation is complete. To pray this prayer is not to distance the transformation from ourselves and think only of it in cosmic terms, to see it referring only to 'the world' and 'them, out there'. It *is* that. But it also presupposes a willingness for a radical, inner transformation of our own lives, which in turn will challenge the families, the communities, the institutions in which we live and work. Praying for the coming of the kingdom

> implies the transformation of human society – its politics, its economics, its personal, group, institutional and international relationships. The Kingdom is not some kind of extraterrestrial entity that will be superimposed on this world. Nor is it a process of 'spiritual' or 'internal' change that will leave the outer realities looking much the same. It is the liberation of the world we live in, know, touch, smell, suffer, from all that corrupts and destroys it . . . That certainly includes the liberation of the individual from all that corrupts him/her. But it goes far beyond that to the rediscovery of the real potential of the whole created order, for that fullness of life in community that the Jews still call 'shalom'.[7]

The transformation which will establish the kingdom will be like the mustard seed, said Jesus, with small beginnings but astonishing growth and ever-widening influence. It begins with the individual and spreads to the group, the community, to society. Small is definitely beautiful here. But it is this radical transformation that we so often flee. Change is painful. We are afraid to risk losing the securities we know even with the promise of deeper security. Do we not see something of our own fear and reluctance reflected in the evasions of the woman at the well as she tried to dodge the real challenge of Jesus and escape into theological argument? Do not our fears resonate with those of Nicodemus as we baulk at the radical change that is tantamount to a new birth?

Jesus said, 'the kingdom of God has come upon you' and we see the effects of that kingdom breaking in upon history in the transformation of Peter, of Mary Magdalene, of Zacchaeus, of Matthew, of the woman taken in adultery, of the woman at the well, and of many whose names are not given us but whose lives were transformed.

We see, too, the resistance to change in the religious leaders of the day, the fear of anything that might challenge the 'status quo' and disturb their complacency. The Prince of Peace comes, bearing the sword of his kingdom, as 'a messenger of peace in a world of strife, and a messenger of strife in a world of false peace' (see below).

To pray, 'Your kingdom come', is to proclaim the victory of God's kingdom over the disintegrative forces of evil – in the realms of healing, politics, exorcism, etc. It is to pray for the release of the power that delivers people from bodily or personality disorders, from mental or psychological disintegration, from physical or social crippling. It is to see the kingdom heralded in the healing of the demoniac, the deaf and dumb, the lepers, the lame, the tax collectors and harlots.

It is to see them going into the kingdom ahead of the self-righteous, ahead of those so hardened by their adherence to the letter of the law that they are now impervious to the spirit of the law, those protected by their own goodness from seeing their dire need. It is to rejoice that those who are prepared to acknowledge their poverty, who cry out from the depths of their shame and degradation, from their human misery and isolation, are able to receive the power that makes whole, that transforms the brokenness and disintegration of lives, that saves and redeems. It is to see this power changing them as startlingly as it once changed water into wine.

Though we pray, 'Your kingdom come', we may be trapped in feelings of powerlessness and futility. Contemplating the world, we see nothing but an appalling mess everywhere – whether it be in the intransigence of governments over racial or financial policies, in the daily spilling of blood in areas dominated by violence, in suffocating corruption in the fields of commerce and high finance, or in the smaller-scale power politics in local councils, industrial management and trade unions, in fields of education and social service, among police, crime squads, or even in the church! Seemingly no area of the world's life is exempt from the decay of corruption – nor, as microcosms of the world, are we.

In the grip of such feelings we need to hold on to the fact

that, in one man, whose life embodied the kingdom by his total obedience to the rule of God, the world *has been changed*. In the life of that man we have seen what it means to pray, 'Your kingdom come'. It may *seem* that the forces of evil are now winning – dragging the whole world with them in a cosmic tug-of-war, but the kingdom has already broken through, the victory already been won. To pray, 'Thy kingdom come' is not the expression of a vague wish, a rather forlorn hope unlikely ever to be fulfilled. It is to affirm the work of Christ; to unite ourselves to it in fervent longing and desire for the consummation of that reign of peace and love and truth which Jesus inaugurated and which he described so vividly in his parables.

O God, who hast given us the grace to carry the sword of thy kingdom of peace, who hast made us messengers of peace in a world of strife, and messengers of strife in a world of false peace, make strong our hand, make clear our voice, give us humility with firmness and insight with passion, that we may fight not to conquer but to redeem.[8]

Into the unholy mess of the world's life we dig a canal by our prayers for the coming of the kingdom. We unblock a little more resistance with each repetition of the Lord's Prayer. Nor is the prayer offered by word alone. With every act of redemptive love that reflects the covenant love of God, we establish the kingdom a little more. In practical terms it means that the love which goes on loving even when it is spurned hastens the coming of the kingdom. The love of parents which follows a beloved child who has inexplicably run away from home, the love of a husband or wife that continues undiminished despite marital infidelity, even repeated infidelity, and that even seeks out and rescues the other from degradation and ruin, the love that lays down its life for a friend, the love that refuses to repay evil with evil – all such loving prays in the kingdom. In such cases of heroic and redemptive loving, which we must all have met from time to time, we have *seen* the kingdom come.

To pray for the completion of the kingdom does not, however, imply waiting in passivity and inaction. The parable of the talents (Matt 18:24ff) makes the clear point that to pray, 'Your kingdom come', means being

up-and-doing, here and now, with the *works* of the kingdom. In such work, the kingdom flashes forth, from the work itself. A cup of cold water is given to one of Christ's little ones and in that unspectacular act, there is a flash – visible to him who has eyes to see – of that glory which signals the dynamic presence and supernatural life of the kingdom.[9]

O God, who hast given us the grace to be the instruments of love in its work of healing and judgment; who hast commissioned us to proclaim forgiveness and condemnation, deliverance to the captive and captivity to the proud, give us the patience of those who understand, and the impatience of those who love, that the might of thy gentleness may work through us, and the mercy of thy wrath may speak through us.[10]

Your will be done

It is not without significance that this phrase comes right at the centre of the prayer. It is the pivotal point on which the rest hinges. And it is this part of the prayer that illustrates how impossible it is for anyone other than a believer to *pray* the Lord's Prayer, no matter how many others may *say* it. For the only way we can pray 'Your will be done' is out of a heart full of love for God. Indeed the test as to whether or not we love God is the extent to which we want *his* will to be done, not our own.

Such a sentiment can slip off the tongue, and flow from the pen, fairly easily, even glibly. It is when we begin to translate it into our actual experience that we have to confess in shame the poverty of our love. For even though we may *say* 'Your will be done', there are many times when we *mean*, '*My* will be done'. Or perhaps we are slightly less blatant (or more self-deceptive, as the case may be) and what it boils down to is, 'Your will be done, providing it conforms to mine.'

We can say 'Your will be done' with relative comfort, when we are expressing a longing for God's will *in general* to be done on earth as in heaven (after all, it would make life so much more tolerable and pleasant all round); but when we have to pray it in the face of some actual situation where his will conflicts utterly with our own hopes, desires, ambitions and longings, then it becomes not a comfortable prayer but a cry of anguish. And that is all right! It is precisely what Jesus himself did in the garden of Gethsemane.

Perhaps we may be surprised that he, who loved God perfectly, could not accept his will with immediate joy – without a murmur. There is no real inconsistency here. To love God so perfectly that there is nothing we want more than his will does not mean that we are blind to the human cost. We still have to face the reality of relinquishing our own wishes, perhaps slowly, bit by bit, through our tears. Our whole longing, because we love God, may be to do his will, but at the crunch point of discovering what it is, we can still paradoxically be filled with that longing while at the same time struggling desperately with the painful implications. In this, Jesus shared our humanity fully. We know that God's will is best and our ultimate happiness lies in following the path of it, but we have to be honest and real at the same time, and accept that we cannot always rid ourselves of the fear involved in stepping out on that path of the unknown which may indeed prove to be the 'way of the cross'. Yes, of course, perfect love will cast out fear, but none of us loves God perfectly – yet.

If I labour this point, it is because I believe there are far too many unnecessary guilt-feelings around when, far from experiencing feelings of glad surrender, people are sometimes initially *appalled* at what the will of God is going to mean for them at a particular stage in their life. But those who step out bravely know the paradoxical inner joy of doing something that humanly-speaking goes right against the grain and hurts deeply, yet carries within it the exciting promise of God's glory and the peace of 'willing one will' with him.

Give us today our daily bread

Here again we are reminded that this is a prayer specifically for the disciples of Jesus. When the crowds followed him hoping he would again provide them with miraculous food (John 6:26) Jesus did not repeat the miracle. Rather he tried to teach them that 'daily bread' was more than the loaves they had eaten previously. 'As the devil had said it would, the distribution of bread moved the crowds to acclaim Jesus as the New Moses, the provider, the Welfare King'[11] for whom they had been waiting, so these words of prayer are not addressed to that wave of enquirers coming to see if this kingdom being preached was for real with all the expected signs. It was for the hard core of his disciples.

It is addressed to the God whose providence supplies needs, and supplies them faithfully. They were to have confidence that the pilgrim people of God would be sustained by him and provided for in all essentials. Their fathers had been fed with manna in the wilderness – on a daily basis. They learnt to be dependent on the God who had called them and chosen them to be his people. In the same way, bread would be supplied to their successors – the new Israel – in *their* pilgrimage.

'Bread' is usually taken to cover the basic necessities of life – adequate food, shelter, clothing, health and security. We have seen how Jesus taught his disciples not to be anxious but to pray for their specific needs to be met. But at once we are faced with the question, 'What constitutes "adequate"?' The interpretation of that word would differ vastly in the West from the Third World. 'Give us this day our daily bread' is therefore pointing to a more searching aspect of the Prayer. It is saying something vital about the politics of Jesus and the Christian ethic of sharing.

I have just returned from the Kalahari Desert where people

readily shared their 'bread' with me – i.e. their food (even though they were on famine relief supplies), their precious water, their humble homes and gave up their beds, rather than allow me to sleep on the floor. To me it seemed movingly generous. But it is also the *norm*. In the desert you share. I was slightly surprised that no one said 'thank you' for the few food supplies I had brought. But, why should they? In the desert no one keeps food to themselves. It is regarded as common property – never '*my* food' but '*our* daily bread' – not to be hoarded or eked out sparingly, but enjoyed *now*, trusting in the providential supply of tomorrow's needs. From a Western background of well-stocked larders and crammed deep freezers, it is hard not to look on this attitude to life as reckless and imprudent. But it comes near to the heart of the kingdom prayer. Maybe that was one of the secrets of the feeding of the five thousand – that in supplying their hunger so bountifully, Jesus recalled people to the pilgrim rule i.e. to share bread rather than sit on a private store ensuring that 'I' and 'mine' do not go hungry no matter what is happening to those outside the family. If people on that occasion were moved to share what food they had, albeit secretly tucked away, as they realised what Jesus was able to do with the total offering of the small boy, then the miracle would have been more than a material one of multiplying food, but a spiritual one of changed hearts and enlarged generosity.

The sharing of bread – especially in a place like the desert – is sacramental. It is a basic Christian principle of economics in the kingdom where we learn the inner meaning of inter-dependence. 'The bread which we break, is it not a *sharing* . . . ?'

I found it thought-provoking that in the Kalahari, where the staple diet is a kind of porridge called 'bogobe', the word used for 'bread' in the Liturgy is the same. The link between daily food and eucharistic food is quite explicit. The bread of the common table and the bread of the altar are one. 'The "bogobe" (porridge) which we break, is it not a sharing of the body of Christ? We who are many are one body, for we all partake of the one "bogobe" (porridge)' (cf. 1 Cor 10:16,17).

'Give *us* . . .' means that 'bread' is a corporate gift to be received and shared corporately. Woe to those who allow Lazarus to go hungry at their gate (Luke 16:19–31). One of the accusations that Eliphaz made (justly or unjustly) against Job was: 'You have given no water to the weary to drink, and you have withheld bread from the hungry . . . You have sent widows away empty, and the arms of the fatherless were crushed' (Job 22:7,9). This was the kind of situation that would be reversed by the revolutionary standards of the kingdom where the Lord would fill 'the hungry with good things', send the rich away empty and 'put down the mighty from their thrones' and exalt the humble and meek (Luke 1:52,53).

Hospitality means an open-handed, open-hearted generosity not crippled by fears or anxieties about whether there will be enough to eat or drink or put on *tomorrow*. 'Give us *today* . . .'

One of the major lessons the Israelites had to learn in the wilderness was trust in the God who would take care of their needs daily. Hoarding turned sour on them and left them with nothing but basketfuls of maggots. To live provisionally – as those provided for – rules out a nervous attitude to life that accumulates a squirrel's hoard against the rainy day that may never come. It teaches us not to amass wealth and possessions, which far from setting us free from anxiety actually add to it, creating a heavy burden and even greater insecurity. Travelling light is essential for the pilgrim – whether crossing Europe with a rucksack or journeying to God.

In the talk (which proved to be his final one) that Thomas Merton gave at the Conference of Abbots and Superiors at Bangkok, he told the story of 'a Buddhist abbot fleeing for his life from a Tibetan monastery before the advance of Communist troops. Another monk had joined him with a train of twenty five yaks loaded with "essential" provisions. The abbot didn't wait with the yaks. While the other monk stayed with his "necessities" and was quickly overtaken by those from whom he was trying to flee, the abbot, leaving everything behind, swam across a river and at last reached India.' How many yaks do we have trailing in our wake?[12]

'Give us today our daily *bread*' – necessities, not luxuries. We who know that our 'bread' is assured and relatively easy to obtain, may well like to pray this part of the Lord's Prayer on behalf of the two thirds of the world that lives below the bread-line. 'Give us', in that context, may well have within it the plea, 'Give *them* by giving *us* the power to live unselfishly, to live by the Christian ethic of sharing and to use whatever influence we have to change economic policies which only succeed in putting more and more bread before the already well-fed, and less and less before the hungry millions. Shatter our illusions and give us a vision of new power structures and policies that will not allow the build-up of butter mountains, rivers of surplus milk and cargo vessels full of rotting wheat destined to be dumped in the ocean. Grant such a deep compassion that the fatuous reasons given for such appalling waste may be seen for what they are, and avenues for getting the food to the needy be found.'

'Give us today our daily bread' seen in this way as, 'Give us, as a global community, the will and the power to see that the world's resources are distributed justly, that agricultural know-how and expertise is made available to all parts of the world, that the fruits of technology are shared,' may well be a prayer that affects the way we vote, that motivates us to lobby our MP on certain issues (as we saw many British Christians do over the Brandt report). It will govern our participation in political rallies in the run-up to a presidential election and our support or not for a particular senator. We have no right to pray this prayer if we are not prepared to work for an 'economy of sharing' and a 'true Christian *common* wealth'.

Bread is the most universal symbol of unity. To eat bread with someone is a sign of fellowship, a bond of friendship, indeed a sacred trust. The Israelites could not slaughter the spies who had infiltrated their strong city by clever deception (Jos 9) because they had broken bread together as part of a covenant relationship. The sacred trust of hospitality was inviolable. The tragedy of the Last Supper was that he who would betray Jesus was prepared to dip with him in the same dish, to sit at the same table and share a meal (Mark 14:20).

No wonder, then, that Jesus used bread as one of the chief symbols in his sacrament of unity. 'The bread which we break, is it not a participation in the body of Christ? . . . we who are many are one body, for we all partake of the one bread' (1 Cor 10:16, 17). Bread broken was to convey his life to his followers, 'I am the bread of life; he who comes to me shall not hunger' (John 6:35). But the bread of life is to be eaten in fellowship signifying our common dependence on God, our essential unity in Christ without distinctions for, in him, 'there is neither Jew nor Greek, there is neither slave nor free, there is neither male nor female' (Gal 3:28).

Just as in the West we grow accustomed to plenty – full larders and well-stocked cupboards – in the realm of the spirit there can be the danger of a supermarket attitude to Jesus, our bread of life, where instead of looking for a daily supply of life-giving sustenance through prayer, reflection upon the scriptures and the sacraments, we expect to 'fill up' occasionally and live off our reserves. But that we cannot do. We are dependent upon fresh bread not stale loaves. We shall be left with 'nothing but a handful of maggots'!

> Break Thou the bread of life,
> Dear Lord, to me.
> As Thou didst break the loaves
> Beside the sea:
> Beyond the sacred page
> I seek Thee, Lord;
> My spirit pants for Thee,
> O living Word![13]

Give us the life-giving food of yourself *today*, Lord, as we break the bread of the table, the bread of your word and the bread of the altar and help us to share readily with one another in that divine spirit of gratuity and liberality in which it is given.

And forgive us our sins . . .

In her book *The Healing Light*, Agnes Sanford speaks very movingly, and very courageously, of a time in her life when she lacked a sense of sin:

> For many years I had been a channel through whom others might receive healing. I knew that this healing included forgiveness – that is, the healing of the personality – the changing of the emotional tenor. At this time I realised that I needed forgiveness, and that forgiveness would restore my emotional balance.
>
> I had thought a great deal about forgiving others, but I had never thought of being forgiven because I was not in the least conscious of sin.
>
> Indeed . . . the one danger of forgiving and healing others without a balancing practice in receiving forgiveness . . . is that . . . [it] closes our eyes to those lingering faults of our human nature that lie deep in the subconscious. It leads directly toward the sin of spiritual pride that is the downfall of most spiritual leaders. However, while I did not know that I needed forgiveness, I knew very well that I needed *something*.[14]

One of the foremost things this part of the Lord's Prayer does for us is to remind us continually of our perpetual need of forgiveness – not only for our 'sins', the wrongdoings and faults for which we can account and take responsibility, but for *sin* and our share in the whole mess and disorder of the world's life of which we are a part. Chaos is that part of the world's life that is organised apart from God, and in all of us there is the chaos that needs redemption. We all need the healing and wholeness that come from forgiveness. Sometimes, in receiving forgiveness, an area deep in our subconscious is healed without our being aware of the sickness or wound that lurked in the depths. Through forgiveness the Lord can unite those bits of ourselves to us that we have disowned – albeit unwittingly.

Yet somehow the whole area of forgiveness is one which people find difficult – whether in the sense of not *feeling* truly repentant, not feeling conscious of sin or not feeling assured that they *are* forgiven.

In his book *Life Together*, Dietrich Bonhoeffer discusses this problem. In the little experimental community he once began, they asked themselves why it was that somehow it seemed to cost very little to confess their sins to God.

Why is it that it is often easier for us to confess our sins to God than to a brother? God is holy and sinless, he is a just judge of evil and the enemy of all disobedience. But a brother is sinful as we are. He knows from his own experience the dark night of secret sin. Why should we not find it easier to go to a brother than to the holy God? But if we do, we must ask ourselves whether we have not been deceiving ourselves with our confession of sin to God, whether we have not rather been confessing our sins to ourselves and also granting ourselves absolution. And is not the reason perhaps for our countless relapses and the feebleness of our Christian obedience to be found precisely in the fact that we are living on self-forgiveness and not a real forgiveness? Self-forgiveness can never lead to a breach with sin; this can be accomplished only by the judging and pardoning Word of God itself.

Who can give us the certainty that, in the confession and the forgiveness of our sins, we are not dealing with ourselves but with the living God? God gives us this certainty through our brother. Our brother breaks the circle of self-deception. A man who confesses his sins in the presence of a brother knows that he is no longer alone with himself; he experiences the presence of God in the reality of the other person . . .

Our brother has been given me that even here and now I may be made certain through him of the reality of God in his judgment and his grace. [15]

Bonhoeffer's community followed quite literally James' exhortation, 'Therefore confess your sins to one another, and pray for one another, that you may be healed' (Jas 5:16).

By whatever means we come to receive the assurance of the Lord's authoritative, 'Go in peace, your sins are forgiven you', we are certainly meant to have that deep inner knowledge and joy. The chaplain of a boy's school told me that on one occasion when a boy had confessed something in the course of a conversation and he had reassured him of God's love and forgiveness, the boy had rushed out of the chapel and turned cartwheels right across the football pitch. The felt certainty of forgiveness does indeed make us want to turn cartwheels of joy, in spirit – even if we are too stiff in the joints to do so physically!

So, not only are we reminded in this part of the Lord's Prayer of the offer of forgiveness, our need to receive it and *experience* its cleansing and healing power, we must surely be reminded, too, of the cost to the Lord in making that forgiveness available. After all, it isn't simply guilt feelings that move us to repent. Plenty of unbelievers live with guilt feelings and are not moved to repentance. Rather, they visit the doctor in search of remedies for the depression or ulcers that perhaps have their origins in guilt. No. It is not primarily guilt but the cross, and the sorrow we feel when we contemplate it, that drives us to our knees. It is the sight of that majestic figure who was despised and rejected, abused and scorned, tortured and crucified because of sin, *our* sin, that makes us feel that if he could be made a public spectacle, then I who helped to put him there can find the courage to expose my shame and own it for what it is.

Each of us finds our own way in the matter of repentance. God leads us and delights when we follow his leading. But we should surely not neglect the rich source of mutual strength and encouragement in 'Body ministry', in allowing a brother or sister in Christ to help us to discover the inner certainty and joy of forgiveness.

The Lord's Prayer, however, reminds us that forgiveness

cannot be earned or deserved. It is free and gratuitous, yet, as we see below, there *are* conditions.

'. . . as we forgive those who sin against us'

Sometimes we may feel stymied at this point, because we cannot, as yet, find it in our hearts to forgive someone who has wronged us. Does that mean we cannot claim God's forgiveness for ourselves? We have looked at one aspect of this in the previous chapter. But we need also to see this part of the Lord's Prayer against its original background which spoke of remitting a debt (the Greek verb is *aphiēmi*). To be accurate, the word *opheilēma* in Greek signifies a monetary debt – in a very literal and materialistic sense. So Jesus was telling his disciples to remit, liberate, forgive a debt, as all Jews were exhorted, indeed compelled, to do in the 'year of jubilee' (Lev 25). No matter how great a debt a man may have run up, in the year of jubilee it was cleared, the slate was wiped clean and everyone began afresh. It meant in practice that moneylenders and many of the rich were loth to lend money and material goods in the penultimate year before the jubilee, knowing that they were unlikely ever to see the return of the loan.

Here Jesus is saying to his disciples, 'With the coming of the kingdom, we enter upon a permanent jubilee in which debts are forgiven, prisoners are set free, land is restored to the poor, things are put right and everyone has the chance to make a fresh start. In the kingdom this is not once every seven years, but every year. For, "the Spirit of the Lord is upon me, because he has anointed me to preach good news to the poor. He has sent me to proclaim release to the captives and recovering of sight to the blind, to set at liberty those who are oppressed, to proclaim the acceptable year of the Lord . . . Today this scripture has been fulfilled in your hearing"' (see Luke 4:18–21).

So the 'Our Father' is 'genuinely a jubilary prayer',[16] an original piece of liberation theology. And what he says here in a nutshell, is borne out in other parts of the gospel where he teaches his disciples to show mercy (Matt 5:7), not to stand on their rights but to live a life of liberality (Matt 5:38–41), to be generous to the one who begs and/or borrows, not looking too anxiously for returns (Matt 5:42) and of course, most poignantly, through the parable of the merciless servant (Matt 18:23–35). Here we have an actual example of jubilee forgiveness.

It is in this way that Jesus' listeners would have understood this part of the prayer.

> Jesus was establishing a strict equation between the practice of the jubilee and the grace of God. He who was not legalist at any other point, and who was ready without hesitation to pardon prostitutes and disreputable people, was nonetheless extremely strict upon one point: 'only he who practices grace can receive grace. The *aphesis* of God toward you becomes vain if you do not practice *aphesis* toward your brethren'[17]

They would have heard it not so much as an injunction to forgive personal injury and hurt but as a prayer for the coming of the kingdom of grace and gratuity where 'earthly, ego-dominated values are turned upside down, so that the dispossessed possess; the have-nots have; the powerless achieve their ambitions; the outcasts are invited in'.[18]

But as Charles Elliott so rightly warns, 'when we reduce prayer for the Kingdom to a political agenda, we are making the Kingdom two-dimensional despite the fact that the consistent theme of Jesus' teaching on the Kingdom is that it is multi-dimensional, involving liberating change at many levels'.[19] This being so, it does not seem to be a misconstruction to see in these words, 'forgive us . . . as we forgive', the grace and pardon we often associate with forgiveness which is not the setting free from actual material or monetary debt, but a liberation of the spirit, an inner freedom. The whole tenor of Jesus' teaching bears out this principle of forgiving freely – not nursing grudges, nor harbouring anger or resentment (Matt 5:22).

'And whenever you stand praying, forgive, if you have anything against any one; so that your Father also who is in heaven may forgive you your trespasses' (Mark 11:25).

Furthermore, as he sought to fulfil the Mosaic law and give it deeper meaning, he said to his disciples, 'You have heard that it was said, "An eye for an eye and a tooth for a tooth." But I say to you, Do not resist one who is evil. But if any one strikes you on the right cheek, turn to him the other also' (Matt 5:38,39). The *lex talionis*, the old law of strict retaliation which permitted the return of an injury in exact proportion to that meted out, was to be superceded by the new law of non-retaliation and non-violence (Matt 5:38–42), turning away wrath, refusing vengeance, transforming hatred by the non-proliferation of evil, forgiving one another as God 'in Christ forgave you' (Eph 4:32).

The old law permitted hatred of the enemy in its understanding of strict justice. 'But I say to you,' said Jesus, 'Love your enemies and pray for those who persecute you.' Only so will you become the inheritors of the kingdom and reach that 'perfection' (Matt 5:48) which is real spiritual maturity.

Lead us not into temptation, but deliver us from evil

Perhaps this is the most difficult part of the Lord's Prayer to comprehend. Are we to suppose that God leads us deliberately into situations of temptation to see if we are strong enough to cope? If so, how could Paul suggest that, with every temptation, God is providing a way of escape (1 Cor 10:13)? That would be to portray God as a contrary God who plays games with us.

We are told in each of the synoptic gospels that Jesus was driven into the wilderness to be tempted (Matt 4:1; Mark 1:12; Luke 4:1,2). It is often pointed out that the Greek verb used here (*peirazō*) has the meaning of putting to the proof as well as tempting, and that the Spirit led Jesus into the wilderness to be proved or tested – for every vision of God, such as he had received in baptism, has to undergo a testing.

Search me out, O God, and know my heart:
put me to the proof and know my thoughts
(Psalm 139:23 NTW)

For him the proving came in the form of temptations to doubt his newly-affirmed Sonship with God, to find those popular, spectacular and easy ways of establishing the kingdom that would eliminate conflict and suffering. But we know how he resisted each temptation. What was actually being tested there in the lonely wastes of the Judean desert, in his silence and his fasting, was his *obedience to the heavenly vision* – his willingness to follow God's call and fulfil his purposes without compromise of any sort, despite the natural, human inclination to shrink from all that such obedience might involve – opposition to the religious leaders of his day, the possibility of being misunderstood, the pain of rejection, the humiliation and horror of arrest, trial and execution. Was he willing to see his mission in terms of the suffering servant Messiah? Would he be able, *throughout* his ministry, to steer a clear course through all the traps and subtle suggestions that could provide escape clauses to suffering? Here in the desert the new Israel was to conquer and succeed where old Israel had failed and been defeated.

At 'Meribah' and 'at Massah in the wilderness' the Israelites had been disobedient (Ps 95:8). They had put God to the test through their unbelief. They had sought to 'prove' God and 'tempt him' even though they had seen his works and really had no need of further proof. In any case, it is for God to try our hearts and to prove us, not the other way round. (Hence Jesus resisted temptation in the wilderness by saying to the devil, 'You shall not tempt the Lord your God', i.e. 'You shall not put him to the test in your unbelief by asking him to prove that he *is* God'.) For that disobedience, the people of God wandered in the wilderness for forty years, and when we look on a map at the probable route of their journey, we see that they wandered in circles.

'Lead us not into temptation' might then be seen to be a prayer to be saved from making the same mistake – from the folly that through hardness of heart, in the face of all God's providence, through unbelief and disobedience, ends up circumnavigating the promised land for years on end (i.e. the promised land of the kingdom and the rich relationship of love and trust with him who is the King.)

There is, however, a secondary aspect of this prayer:

> We know that God leads us into situations in which we can serve him and do his will. *This* is certainly his purpose. But every situation into which he may lead us, holds within itself temptations for us. Our temptation, always, lies in a simple choice we must make; the choice between service to God and disservice to God. He cannot open up to us an opportunity of service without opening up to us an opportunity of disservice. In the light of this clear fact we can see how God cannot lead us into any place where we can serve him without leading us into temptation.[20]

God is not intentionally seeking to trip us up. He longs that we should glorify his name through holy and obedient lives, but he cannot create artificial, hot-house circumstances in which to do this. Our obedience is to be offered within the context of the real world, and that means accepting life as it comes to us, and *will* always come to us in an imperfect world, with all its temptations.

James has pointed out: 'Let no one say when he is tempted, "I am tempted by God"; for God cannot be tempted with evil and he himself tempts no one' (Jas 1:13). We can be perfectly sure of two things. God stands alongside us in temptation to strengthen us. He is on our side. His overcoming power is available and there for the asking. But we do have to ask for it. There is nothing automatic or magical about receiving grace. He wants us to be warriors in the fight. He will not be like a mother who always rushes in to defend her child in his or her battles, never allowing the child to develop in strength, selfhood and maturity.

Secondly, as has been observed earlier in this book, each success, each victory over temptation will both strengthen us for the next but also ensure that there *is* a next. The more we seek to do God's will, the more perfect we become in obedience, the more temptations are likely to increase. The devil does not give up easily. We are told that after forty days he departed from the wilderness and left Jesus. But for how long? He surely only withdrew in order to gather more force for the next onslaught, like a wave retreating in order to advance and crash upon the shore in endlessly repeating waves.

This need not daunt us, however, for we know that God is a deliverer who delivers us from evil. Therefore the Lord exhorts us to make this petition for deliverance. For he will save us, not so much by coddling us and ensuring that we never have to meet evil head-on in spiritual warfare, in subtle temptation and perhaps in demonic force. He is not advocating a form of Christian escapism. Rather he is asking us to recognise our awful pride which makes us attempt the impossible – which makes us tackle evil in our own strength. God will and does help us to face evil and to master it by arming us for battle and giving us the inner resources. But our armour has to be claimed piece by piece, and put on with prayer (Eph 6:11–18). The Lord does not deliver us from evil by protecting us from confrontation any more than he did for his Son. He delivers us from defeat by it, he delivers us *out* of evil and brings us safely to the victory side. The words of the psalmist ring with the confidence we can all know in times of spiritual battle for, at such times, God can be to *us* our strength, our crag, our fortress, our deliverer whom we love, our shield and mighty saviour and our high defence.

> He reached down from on high and took me:
> he drew me out of the great waters.
> He delivered me from my strongest enemy:
> from my foes that were mightier than I.
> They confronted me in the day of calamity:
> But the Lord was my upholder.
> He brought me out into a place of liberty:
> and rescued me because I delighted his heart.
>
> (Ps 18:16–19 NTW)

13

'WATCH AND PRAY' – the prayer of readiness

Watch and pray that you may not enter into temptation.
(Mark 14:38)

We can hardly leave the subject of being delivered out of
temptation and girding on the weapons of spiritual warfare
without pausing to consider that other way of withstand-
ing temptation that Jesus enjoined upon his disciples in
Gethsemane: 'Watch and pray that you may not enter into
temptation' (Mark 14:38).

For them, as we well know, the spirit was indeed willing but
the flesh weak. They were able neither to watch nor pray.
Instead, they slept.

'Temptation' here has the particular connotation of tribulation. In Jesus the kingdom has been inaugurated. All the
events of the Lord's ministry are 'eschatological' events and
he recognises in the attack about to be made on himself and
his disciples, the approach of the greater tribulation of which
he had warned them (Matt 24; Mark 13). They are about to be
put through a particular and immediate testing time, the
precursor of the 'fiery ordeal' of which Peter speaks (1 Peter
4:12), and other forms of trial that would befall the youthful church. For this is how the church must have understood
these words as it later entered into the tribulation of
persecution.

There are two main 'watching' themes in the gospels.
Firstly, there is the watching and waiting for the coming of
the Lord (the waiting servants, the thief in the night, the

ten virgins) and secondly there is the being alert and prepared for testing.

Originally, Jesus' injunction to watch was not only intended to warn his hearers to be prepared for the enemy within but also for the enemy without – the inevitable and impending crisis that would result from his ministry. Later, when 'the immediate crisis passed, the parables [about watching] were naturally reapplied to the situation in which the early Christians found themselves after the death of Jesus'.[1]

Yet all the sayings advocating readiness and the wisdom of being prepared, even if adapted and given particular application by the early church, have an immediate relevance within the context of the ministry of Jesus. Through them he appealed to men to recognise that the kingdom of God had broken into human history and that the coming of that kingdom brought with it a tremendous crisis in which they would be judged as wise or foolish, faithful or unfaithful.

How then were the disciples to ensure this 'readiness', first for the possible tribulation and then for the return of the Lord at a time when they least expected him?

'Let your loins be girded and your lamps burning,' said Jesus, 'and be like men who are waiting for their master . . . Blessed are those servants whom the master finds awake when he comes' (Luke 12:35–37). 'Girding up the loins' to a Jew meant gathering up the skirts of his garment and tucking them into his belt in order to secure greater freedom of movement – especially rapid movement such as running. It became the idiomatic way of saying, 'Be ready for action.' In other words, the watching disciple would be one who was alert, 'on his toes', prepared for anything – not like a servant slacking off in his master's absence confident that there would always be time for eleventh-hour preparation.

Lamps were to be burning – not just trimmed and ready, but actually alight (clear echoes here of the parable of the ten virgins). Even the time it took to light an oil lamp could be crucial – those very minutes could coincide with the arrival of the master. It is powerful picture-language. We can scarcely fail to grasp the sense of urgency in it.

In the parable of the ten virgins, we might be tempted to think the five wise maidens were also rather selfish ones. Was it not pretty mean to refuse to share their oil with the foolish? Did it not conflict with the teaching of Jesus elsewhere about giving to those who beg, and lending to those who ask to borrow (Matt 5:42)?

The point, however, is that we may be able to share with others our food, our material possessions, our worldly wealth – but we cannot share our readiness. Readiness is a matter of *personal* preparation, a possession of the soul that each must cultivate individually. We cannot 'borrow' another's readiness, nor hold ourselves in readiness for another vicariously. Even if the early church understood the teaching about watching and waiting as a call to corporate readiness for the Lord's return (which they believed to be imminent), the sum total of that readiness could only be made up of individual fidelities, the individual girt loins and burning lamps.

Individual readiness comes about through watching and praying – not being sluggish or apathetic in discipleship, nor rushing around wasting spiritual energy, but leaving space to listen to God, equipping ourselves for battle and waiting to see *his* victories. 'In quietness and in trust shall be your strength', said Isaiah to Hezekiah in the face of national crisis (Isa 30:15). 'Fear not, stand firm, and see the salvation of the Lord', said Moses to his fearful people (Exod 14:13). Only in watching, only in standing still, only in the quietness of a trustful heart can the disciple be awake to the signs of the kingdom wherever they are to be found. Only so can he welcome every intimation of the kingdom's presence. And, 'kingdom-awareness' comes through prayer and meditation, where we learn to discern the signs of the times, to listen to the prophetic voices that speak forth into contemporary situations, to cooperate with the transforming power of the Spirit. It comes in waiting upon God in eager expectation that he will act, and act savingly.

One of the most vivid pictures given us of this kind of waiting is found in the parable of the wedding garment (Matt 22:1–14). Perhaps it seems strangely unjust to our Western minds? A guest is given a last-minute invitation to a wedding feast and then, with no time to make suitable preparations and therefore forced to come just as he is, he is condemned for not appearing suitably dressed for the occasion.

But surely, the thrust of this particular parable is the urgent need for constant readiness for the heavenly banquet? No matter when, or how suddenly, the invitation comes to attend the feast, the one who lives in a permanent state of readiness will be wearing the right garment. By prayer and service, praise and penitence, he will be clothed in righteousness. So often in scripture, a right relationship with God is described in terms of clothing. He who comes within the sphere of the kingdom's activity will be given 'the mantle of praise instead of a faint spirit' (Isa 61:3). The wonder of being in a covenant relationship with God leads the prophet to cry out, 'I will greatly rejoice in the Lord . . . for he has clothed me with the garments of salvation, he has covered me with a robe of righteousness' (Isa 61:10). The Lord's priests are to be clothed with righteousness (Ps 132:9). Those who are unfaithful are those whose garments have been stripped from them (Ezekiel 16:37; 23:26; Isa 47:2,3; Hosea 2:3,9,10; Amos 2:16), but those who are worthy are robed in white (Rev 3:4). The waiting church is like a bride adorned for her bridegroom. She will be 'clothed with fine linen, bright and pure – for fine linen is the righteous deeds of the saints' (Rev 19:7,8; 21:2).

The garment of readiness, therefore, is prayer, a garment which we must needs wrap around ourselves perpetually for this is the garment of *his* righteousness which replaces 'the filthy rags' of our own, those unsuitable robes which would make our presence at the marriage feast a scandal to others and a judgment to ourselves.

> O great absolver, grant my soul may wear
> The lowliest garb of penitence and prayer,
> That in the Father's courts my glorious dress
> May be the garment of thy righteousness.[2]

APPENDIX

PRACTICAL SUGGESTIONS – a follow-up to some of the chapters

Chapter 1

Two suggestions to encourage the use of our senses as an aid to centring down and becoming still.

A silent walk

Go for a walk alone, or if in company, in silence.
Be aware of the ground beneath your feet. What is it – earth, shingle, gravel, mud, tarmac, pine needles, grass? If appropriate (e.g. on the beach) go barefooted the better to feel the sand, grass, etc.
Listen to the sounds around . . . near or distant, human or animal, elemental or mechanical, traffic or machines.
See shapes, colours, textures . . . near at hand, in the middle distance or far off. Choose a particular colour, and concentrate on noticing the many shades of it. Choose a particular shape, e.g. a curve, look for all the ways in which it appears, and the variations on it. Alternate between objects of natural beauty and man-made objects, e.g. the architecture of houses, fences and gates, monuments and carvings. Look closely for insects, and study their colours and shapes. Look closely at people and see what their outward appearance and body language tell you about them.
Touch wood, stone, petals, brickwork, shells, grass, animals

. . . especially their fur. Dip your hands in water. Feel the texture of wool, silk, the barks of trees, etc.

Smell country smells, such as a farmyard, milking shed, stables, new-mown hay, freshly-baked bread; flowers – in the woods, in churches, in homes and in the florists; city smells – wet pavements after a shower, smells from restaurants, libraries, post offices, hardware shops, supermarkets, hairdressers, leather goods.

Taste. If you normally eat quickly, or in a great hurry, or with many interruptions, plan for a meal when it is possible to eat slowly and sit to enjoy and savour every item of food. Don't start getting the next course when you are still chewing the last mouthful of the one before. Pause and be leisurely. It's good for the digestion and the figure as well as prayer!

A spiritual anthology

Keep a collection of photos, picture postcards, drawings and paintings of beautiful scenes, sculptures or carvings. If these are mounted, a suitable quotation may be written alongside.

Such an anthology enables us to enter into the wonders of nature even when circumstances make it impossible to enjoy them at first hand. We can 'see, hear, touch, taste and smell' from our fireside chairs, our desks or the kitchen table with the use of memory, through which we can recall an experience and savour it more fully at our leisure.

It is helpful to divide the anthology into sections, and to use a ring-leaf folder so that it can be added to as you wish.

Chapter 2

Seeking Solitude

Book a time in your diary to be alone, and regard it as a firm commitment. All too often we feel selfish about refusing a request or declining an engagement which clashes with that time. We allow it to be eroded if not completely swallowed up. We mustn't. It is time which we have promised to God, and that is sufficient reason for turning down all conflicting demands upon it.

Book a place – if at all possible, away from home and all the reminders of those things 'we have left undone, which we ought to have done' It may be a Retreat House, a room in a local church or in the home of a friend, or the open air (when weather permits). Avoid reading too much, but take the opportunity to *listen* – to the noise inside oneself, to what the world is saying, but chiefly to God.

Reflect back at the end of the retreat on any ideas, feelings or thoughts that seemed important and may need follow-up. Make the final hour of solitude one of prayerful stillnes and thankfulness.

Increase the length of the times of solitude as opportunity allows, arriving at an eventual retreat day, weekend or longer.

The following help to those making a first retreat was first written by Sister Cyrilla csmv for the Community journal, *Fiat* (no longer published). It is printed here as a suggestion to those looking for assistance in their first venture into solitude.

A first retreat

There are many ways of making a retreat, each with its own merits. But there has to be a first time for everything, and the ordinary Christian addresses himself to the business with some of the feelings of a new-made knight approaching the unfamiliar territory of the wild greenwood . . . There is no way of knowing but by trying. He can be sure that he will leave it in the end a far richer and a wiser man. The great necessity is to enter the retreat and stay in it until it is over, for the love of God.

Certain actions and dispositions will undoubtedly help him on his way.

The first is silence, the attention of the listening heart, to be kept as strictly as possible.

The second is bodily stillness and gentleness, not to be 'busily seeking continual change'.

The third is nature – look at the face of the country around you. If this is unbearable, look at the sky – it is full of variety.

The fourth is song – listen in your inmost heart to music, if you have that faculty. 'Heard melodies are sweet, but those unheard are sweeter' – happy those who have both!

The fifth is to make something beautiful for God's glory.

> God hath no better praise,
> And man in his hasty days
> is honoured for them.

The sixth is to think of the people we know, and practise loving them.

The seventh is to look at our lives, as they have been and as they are now, and thank God heartily for them.

The eighth is to grieve for our sins and those of all the world.

The ninth is to remember that Jesus said, 'I am the truth', and to determine to love and desire and follow that truth for ever.

The tenth is to be full of joy because God made me and loves me and invites me to live with him for eternity.

This scheme will not appeal to all. Some, for example, will feel an urgent need of strenuous exercise or severe study or penitential practices. They may well be right – God leads his own by his own ways. The great thing is, however, to observe the programme laid down by whoever is in charge of the retreat.

The recommendations given above are not meant to be practised in chronological or any other order, or all at once. They are meant to relax, not to tighten our bonds. They take no account of God's uncovenanted mercies. The new-made knight may find at the end that he has received a revelation that will transform his whole life – this can happen. Or it may not. He is there, seated firmly on his horse (his humanity), with the weapons of a Christian in his hands, in complete readiness to accept whatever falls to his lot, content because he knows more and more surely from whose hands it comes.

Those who have never tried the experience will speak of this silence as artificial or unnatural. It is the endless chatter of needless talk that strikes the man/woman who has just come from Retreat as artificial and unnatural. But the majority shrink from the experience. Silence reveals the soul that is in them, and they are not at home with their soul. Silence is the hand of God besetting them before and behind, and they cannot endure that touch of the spiritual life . . . Some there are that have no silence, and that kill the silence around them . . .

At last the little human heart, so full to bursting with its own selfhood, so madly preoccupied with its baubles, so greedy of ease and comfort, is purged of its idols and disciplined to a great silence. It waits, and it has not long to wait; for 'Thy opening and His entering are but one moment, and to wait until thou openest is harder for him than for thee.'

(E. Herman, *The Meaning and Value of Mysticism* [James Clarke, 1915], pp. 127, 129)

Chapter 5

A meditative intercession on the word

The debased word

Lord, you have given us power to communicate through words, but we have
  – misused and devalued them
  – overloaded and squandered them
  – used them as barriers and sheltered behind them to avoid the truth.

In a world heavily influenced by the media, make us alert to words that would
- cheapen
- flood
- manipulate
- the smooth word of propaganda; the persuasive word that would rob us of right judgment.

Forgive us
- the divisions of the searing word
- words spoken in heat and anger
- barbed words
- unspoken words that fester inside
- the wordiness of words that stifle relationships.

'Therefore, wait for me, says the Lord, for the day when I arise . . . yea, at that time, I will change the speech of the peoples to a pure speech . . .'

The hidden word

Lord, give us
. . . receptivity to hear those who speak without words
- the dumb
- the autistic
- the inarticulate
- the creatures who share the earth with us

. . . and the sensitivity to be attuned to
- the silent voices of the persecuted
- the cries of those trapped in their own isolation
- the language of tears.

Lead us to a right expectation of words, so that,
'We are not disappointed at the end of our travels because we were expecting the wrong things . . .
Where man expects a thing, God provides a person . . .
The Word within a word, unable to speak a word,
swaddled with darkness.'

The confessed word

We give thanks for the gift of words, and pray for all who are
called to use them
- in witness and confession of faith
- in prophecy and teaching
- in healing and consolation
- in public proclamation and private counselling
- in writing and printing.

We pray for those who teach others to use words.

'In the beginning was the Word' – the active, creative
Spirit, in all things and before all things. All our words may
have significance and dignity as servants of the Word.

Lord, grant us to be disciplined in everyday speech that
Every phrase and sentence is right, every word is at home,
    Taking its place to support the others,
    The word neither diffident nor ostentatious,
    The easy commerce of the old and the new,
    The common word exact without vulgarity,
    The formal word precise but not pedantic,
    The complete consort dancing together
Every phrase and every sentence an end and a beginning.

The revealed word

    'Jesus of Nazareth, the Word with which God has broken
his silence.'

Give thanks for the inspiration of the long line of prophets
who spoke forth the word of the Lord at great personal cost;
for the poor of Israel waiting in expectation for that Word
who was to be their consolation; and for Mary, chiefest
of their number, 'the selfless space in which God became
man . . . the silence in which his Word can be heard'.

'He called forth a purity so great that within this transparency,
He would concentrate Himself to the point of appearing as a
child.'

'And the Word was made flesh and dwelt among us . . . and
we beheld his glory . . . full of grace and truth.'

(First produced as intercessions for csmv by Sister Bridget Mary and Sister Margaret Magdalen)

Meditation on the scriptures

Many people have found a fresh experience of meditation upon the scriptures through the *Spiritual Exercises* of St Ignatius of Loyola.

For a long time, the use of the imagination has been discouraged in prayer, and thought to be a distraction. This has denied us an important way not simply of understanding the scriptures with our minds, but experiencing them in our hearts, entering into them at the feeling level, learning to be present to the Lord in his Word and hearing it addressed to us now, individually and specifically. Teresa of Avila was a great advocate of the use of the imagination in prayer, and in the *Spiritual Exercises* of Ignatius we are able to recover this way into the scriptures with all the fruit and fresh insight it reveals.

The language of the *Spiritual Exercises* may be dated (and may need 'translation' into contemporary terms, which David L. Fleming SJ has sought to do: See, *A Contemporary Reading of the Spiritual Exercises* (Chicago: Institute of Jesuit Sources). The value of the practice is, however, timeless.

For the full version of the *Spiritual Exercises*, see, Louis Puhl SJ, *The Spiritual Exercises of Ignatius* (Chicago: Loyola University Press, 1951).

Chaim Potok

Chaim Potok has written a number of novels which provide a picture of the life and early training of Orthodox Jews. Among them are:
> *The Chosen* (Penguin, 1970);
> *The Promise* (Penguin, 1969);
> *My Name is Asher Lev* (Penguin, 1974);
> *In the Beginning* (Penguin, 1976);
> *Wanderings* (Hutchinson, 1979).

NOTES

Introduction: A portrait of Jesus – the man of prayer

1 Andrew Murray, *The Ministry of Intercession* (James Nisbet, 1898), p. 132.
2 Alan Ecclestone, *Yes to God* (Darton, Longman and Todd, 1975).
3 Attributed to Richard Rolle.
4 Rowan Williams, *The Wound of Knowledge* (Darton, Longman and Todd, 1979), p. 111.
5 Andrew Murray, *The Ministry of Intercession*, p. 136.
6 Mother Mary Clare SLG, cited from a paper delivered to members of Religious Communities, 1973.
7 Andrew Murray, *The Ministry of Intercession*, p. 136.
8 Taken from the Brakkenstein Community of Holland's *Rule for a New Brother* (ET: Darton, Longman and Todd, 1973), pp. 33–34.

Chapter 1 'Consider the lilies'

1 Thomas Verny, *The Secret Life of the Unborn Child* (Sphere Books, 1981).
2 Elizabeth Moberly, 'A Marian Trilogy' (unpublished).
3 Evelyn Underhill, *Practical Mysticism* (New York: E. P. Dutton and Co. Inc., 1943), p. 90.
4 Michel Quoist, *Prayers of Life* (Gill and Macmillan, 1963), pp. 3–4.
5 Richard Foster, *Meditative Prayer* (Marc Europe, 1983), p. 21.
6 Julian of Norwich, *Revelations of Divine Love* chapter 44 (Penguin Books, 1966), p. 130.
7 A. M. Hunter, *Introducing New Testament Theology* (SCM Press, 1957). Italics mine.
8 ibid., p. 18.
9 See David Runcorn, *Silence*, Grove Spirituality Series 16 (Grove Booklets, 1986), p. 20.
10 Icons in the Eastern Orthodox Church are paintings or mosaics of saints, biblical characters or divine mysteries (Greek *eikon*, image).

The iconographer follows definite rules in the art which affect the line, shapes, symbolic colours, etc.

Icons are not pictures to be looked *at* but, as it were, windows to be looked *through*. By the very discipline of iconography, they have the power to draw the believer *into* the mystery they depict. They are therefore reverenced by Orthodox worshippers.

Here I am suggesting that God can use some of the everyday scenes around us in the same way – speak to us through them and, by this prayer through the eyes, enable us to penetrate something of the mystery of suffering. '. . . the artistic perfection of an ikon [is] not only a reflection of the celestial glory – it is a concrete example of matter restored to its original harmony and beauty, and serving as a vehicle of the Spirit. The ikons [are] part of the transfigured cosmos,' Nicholas Zernov, *The Russians and their Church* (SPCK, 1945), p. 108.

11 Rev. B. T. Davies. From a sermon preached in St Mary's Convent Chapel, Wantage on Lent 4, 1986.

12 In her book *Chasing the Dragon* (Hodder and Stoughton, 1980), Jackie Pullinger describes walking around the city of Hong Kong – sometimes for a whole day – praying in the Spirit. Other Christians have also used this form of prayer as a way of claiming territory for the Lord and proclaiming the Lordship of Jesus over situations which, humanly-speaking, seem hopeless and in which they themselves feel helpless.

13 Alan Amos, interviewed in *Grassroots* magazine, February 1983. Cited in David Runcorn, *Silence*, p. 15.

14 William Johnston, *Christian Mysticism Today* (Collins, 1984), p. 54.

15 John Wesley, *Sermons on Several Occasions* (Epworth Press, 1971), p. 301.

16 Cited in David Runcorn, *Silence*, p. 12.

17 John Drury, *Angels and Dirt* (Darton, Longman and Todd, 1972).

18 Michel Quoist, *Prayers of Life*, p. 10.

19 Source unknown.

20 Thomas Merton, *Thoughts in Solitude* (Burns and Oates, 1958), p. 91.

21 Richard Jefferies, *The Story of My Heart* (Longmans, 1907), pp. 14, 15, 17.

22 A key theme in the spirituality of St Ignatius of Loyola, see his *Spiritual Exercises*.

23 H. Bonar, 'Fill thou my life, O Lord my God', *Hymns Ancient and Modern (Revised)* (William Clowes and Sons, Ltd, 1950), No 373.

24 Anne Long, *Approaches to Spiritual Direction*, Grove Spirituality Series 9 (Grove Booklets, 1984), p. 6.

25 Teilhard de Chardin, *Le Milieu Divin* (Collins, 1957), pp. 36–37.

26 Esther de Waal, *Seeking God* (Fount, 1984), p. 105.

27 Richard Foster, *Celebration of Discipline* (Hodder and Stoughton, 1978), p. 1.

28 Esther de Waal, *Seeking God*, p. 103.

29 Martin Buber, *Hasidism and Modern Man* (New York: Harper Torch Books, 1958), p. 162.
30 Cf. Robert M. Grant and David Noel Freedman, *The Secret Sayings of Jesus according to the Gospel of Thomas* (Fontana, 1960), p. 111.
31 William Temple, *Nature, Man and God* (Macmillan, 1934), p. 491.
32 Stephen Verney, *Water into Wine* (Fount, 1958), p. 180.
33 John Greenleaf Whittier, 'Dear Lord and Father of mankind', *The English Hymnal* (OUP, 1906), No 383.
34 Gregory of Nyssa, *The Life of Moses*, trans. A. J. Malherbe, E. Ferguson, Classics of Western Spirituality (Paulist Press, 1978), p. 95.

Chapter 2   'To a lonely place'

1 Henri Nouwen, *Out of Solitude* (Ave Maria Press, 1974), p. 21.
2 Madame Guyon, *A Method of Prayer*, trans. Dugald Macfadyen (James Clark, 1902), chapter 16.
3 Thomas Merton, *The Sign of Jonas* (Burns and Oates, 1961), p. 304.
4 Gerard Hughes, *In Search of a Way* (E. J. Dwyer, 1978), pp. 41–42.
5 John Greenleaf Whittier, 'Dear Lord and Father of mankind', *The English Hymnal* (OUP, 1906), No 383.
6 Rainer M. Rilke, *Book of Pilgrimage*, further details unknown.
7 Richard Foster, *Meditative Prayer* (Marc Europe, 1983), p. 9.
8 See Eithne Wilkins, *The Rose-garden Game* (Gollancz, 1969), p. 87.
9 'Centring down' is a term often used of the process of collecting oneself, gathering together one's 'scatteredness'. Dr Victor Demant has pointed out that 'because of the fall . . . a man becomes ec-centric (i.e. drawn away from his centrality)'. In prayer we reverse the effects of the fall and withdraw to the centre of our beings, return to the heart. We enter the depths of our souls, become unified, recollected, absorbed and attentive to God.
10 A. W. Tozer, *The Pursuit of God* (Kingsway, 1982), p. 43.
11 Henri Nouwen, *Out of Solitude*, pp. 21–22.
12 See Thomas Merton, *The Climate of Monastic Prayer*, p. 35.
13 Mother Mary Clare SLG, cited from a paper given privately to Religious Communities, 1973.
14 Henri Nouwen, *Reaching Out* (Fount, 1980), p. 60.
15 William Johnston, *Christian Mysticism Today* (Collins, 1984), p. 54.
16 James Thurber, cited by Wendy Robinson in *Exploring Silence* Fairacres Publication 36 (SLG Press, 1974), p. 9.
17 C. G. Jung. Source unknown.
18 Wendy Robinson, *Exploring Silence*, p. 9.
19 Thomas Merton, *The Sign of Jonas*, p. 262.
20 Benjamin Whichcote, *Select Aphorisms* (Christian Tract Society, 1822) p. 150.

21 W. H. Vanstone, *The Stature of Waiting* (Darton, Longman and Todd, 1982).
22 Dr M. Zernov, from her translation of the Tula resumé by N. I. Troitzky (Russia, 1911) on the icon 'Jesus Christ the Perfect Silence'.
23 Patrick Grant, *A Dazzling Darkness* (Fount, 1985), p. 66.
24 Ramon Lull, *A Book of the Lover and the Beloved* (SPCK, 1923), p. 24.
25 James Finley, *Merton's Palace of Nowhere* (Ave Maria Press, 1978), cited on p. 61.
26 John Ruysbroeck, *The Sparkling Stone* (J. M. Dent and Sons Ltd, 1916), pp. 186–187.

Chapter 3 'Abba'

1   Donald Coggan, *The Prayers of the New Testament* (Hodder and Stoughton, 1967), p. 19.
2   A. W. Tozer, *The Pursuit of God* (Kingsway, 1982), p. 43.
3   Joachim Jeremias, *The Prayers of Jesus* (SCM Press, 1967), p. 109.
4   ibid.
5   ibid., p. 111.
6   A. W. Tozer, *The Pursuit of God*, p. 50.
7   Gerard Hughes, *God of Surprises* (Darton, Longman and Todd, 1985), p. 21.
8   Donald Coggan, *The Prayers of the New Testament*, p. 21.
9   C. S. Lewis, *Letters to Malcolm Chiefly on Prayer* (Fount, 1977), p. 15.
10 Julian of Norwich, *Revelations of Divine Love* chapter 77 (Penguin Books, 1966), p. 200.
11 Nicholas Zernov, 'Explanatory notes' of *A Manual of Eastern Orthodox Prayers* (SPCK, 1968), p. x.
12 See Thomas Merton, *The New Man* (Burns and Oates, 1962), especially the chapter entitled 'Free Speech', pp. 46–54.
13 Julian of Norwich, *Revelations of Divine Love* chapter 59, p. 167.
14 Isaac of Stella, *Isaac de l'Etoile, Sermons 1* ed. A. Hoste and G. Salet (Paris: Sources Chretiennes, 1967), Sermon 5, pp. 122–127.

Chapter 4 'As his custom was'

1   For material relating to Jewish liturgy, see Joachim Jeremias, *The Prayers of Jesus* (SCM Press, 1967), pp. 66–72.
2   James Finley, *Merton's Palace of Nowhere* (Ave Maria Press, 1978), p. 29.

3 Joachim Jeremias, *The Prayers of Jesus*, p. 74. The brackets, reproduced here from the original, indicate later additions.
4 Christian Celebration, *Catholic Quarterly*, 1973.

Chapter 5 'As it is written'

1 A phrase used in David Runcorn, *Silence*, Grove Spirituality Series 16 (Grove Booklets, 1986), p. 12.
2 Letter of St Ignatius to the Magnetians.
3 T. S. Eliot, 'Gerontion' *The Collected Poems 1909–1962* (Faber and Faber Ltd, 1963), p. 39.
4 A. M. Hunter, *Introducing New Testament Theology* (SCM Press, 1957), p. 15.
5 D. Bonhoeffer, *Psalms*, Fairacres Publication 81 (SLG Press, 1982), p. 3.
6 ibid., p. 8.
7 See André Louf, *Teach Us to Pray* (Darton, Longman and Todd, 1974), especially the chapter entitled 'Rocking and Chewing the Word', pp. 46–47.
8 ibid., p. 47.
9 Dr Maurice Williams, from an article first published in *Fiat* 6 (1983), the now defunct journal of the Community of St Mary the Virgin.
10 Brakkenstein Community, *Rule for a New Brother: The Spiritual Life* (Darton, Longman and Todd, 1973), p. 52.
11 Juan Carlos Ortiz, *Call to Discipleship* (New Jersey: Logos International), p. 91.
12 Brakkenstein Community, *Rule for a New Brother*, p. 48.

Chapter 6 'I have prayed for you'

1 Henri Nouwen, *The Genesee Diary* (New York: Image Books, 1981), p. 145.
2 Edward Farrell, *Prayer is a Hunger* (Sheed and Ward, 1974), p. 83.
3 Henri Nouwen, *The Genesee Diary*, p. 145.
4 Elizabeth Goudge, *Green Dolphin Country* (Hodder and Stoughton, 1944), p. 359.
5 Martin Israel, *Summons to Life* (Hodder and Stoughton, 1974), p. 76.
6 James Finley, *Merton's Palace of Nowhere* (Ave Maria Press, 1978), p. 29.
7 Fr Matta El-Meskeen, *Directions on Prayer* (St Mark, Monthly Review of the Monastery of St Macarius, Nov 1985), p. 2.
8 Henri Nouwen, *Reaching Out* (Fount, 1980), p. 60.

9 Thomas Merton, *New Seeds of Contemplation* (New York: New Dimensions, 1961).
10 Fr Matta El-Meskeen, *Directions on Prayer*, pp. 3 and 2.
11 Donald Coggan, *Prayers of the New Testament* (Hodder and Stoughton, 1967), p. 71.

Chapter 7 'Glorify your name'

1 Maisie Spens, *Concerning Himself* (Hodder and Stoughton, 1937), p. 53.
2 Susan Lenkes (cited in Lenten Readings produced by St Michael's Church, Summertown, N. Oxford, 1985).
3 Maisie Spens, *Concerning Himself*, p. 53.
4 ibid.
5 A Cistercian Monk, *The Hermitage Within* (Darton, Longman and Todd, 1977), p. 26.
6 Dag Hammarskjöld, *Markings* (Faber and Faber, 1960), p. 110.
7 Frank Cooke, *Jesus* (Scripture Union, 1984), p. 41.
8 Martin Buber, *Hasidism and Modern Man* (New York: Harper Torch Books, 1958), pp. 199 and 81.
9 Walter Eichrodt, *Ezekiel* (ET: SCM Press, 1970), p. 555.
10 Charles Wesley, 'Love Divine, all loves excelling', *The English Hymnal* (OUP, 1906), No 437.
11 From a sermon preached by Rev. Basil Davies in St Mary's Convent Chapel, at Lent 4, 1986.
12 Fr Matta El-Meskeen, *The Mystic's Prayer Rite* (St Mark, Monthly Review of the Monastery of St Macarius, November 1985), p. 6.
13 A Russian word for an old man. In the Eastern Orthodox Church the title is given to a monk who has received from the Holy Spirit gifts of wisdom, discernment and counsel.
14 Irina Gorninov, *The Message of St Seraphim*, Fairacres Publication 26 (SLG Press, 1972), p. 12.
15 A. M. Allchin, *The World is a Wedding* (Darton, Longman and Todd, 1978), p. 88.
16 Corrie ten Boom (with John and Elizabeth Sherrill), *The Hiding Place* (Hodder and Stoughton, 1971).
17 Sister Kirsty, *The Choice* (Hodder and Stoughton, 1982), p. 190.
18 Metropolitan Anthony Bloom, 'Body and Matter in the Spiritual Life' in A. M. Allchin (ed), *Sacrament and Image. Essays in Christian Understanding of Man* (1967), p. 40 – cited in *Seasons of the Spirit*, Every, Harries and Ware (SPCK, 1984), p. 220.
19 The Orthodox hymn for the Feast of Transfiguration, from *The Festal Menaion* p. 467, cited in *Seasons of the Spirit*, Every, Harries and Ware, p. 221.

20   The collect for Lent 4, *The Alternative Service Book 1980* (Hodder and Stoughton, 1980), p. 517.

Chapter 8   'Father, forgive them'

1   Andrew Elphinstone, *Freedom, Suffering and Love* (SCM Press, 1976), pp. 137–138.
2   Petru Dumitriu, *Incognito* (William Collins and Sons Ltd, 1962), pp. 382–383.
3   ibid., p. 354.
4   Andrew Elphinstone, *Freedom, Suffering and Love*, p. 128.
5   ibid., p. 57.
6   Sir Cecil Spring Rice, 'I vow to thee my country', *Hymns Ancient and Modern (Revised)* (William Clowes and Sons, Ltd, 1950), No 579.
7   See Stephen Verney, *Water into Wine* (Fount, 1985), p. 179.
8   Source unknown.

Chapter 9   'My God, why have you forsaken me?'

1   John White, *People in Prayer* (IVP, 1977), p. 151.
2   C. S. Lewis, *A Grief Observed* (Faber and Faber Ltd, 1966), p. 7, 8.
3   Maria Boulding, *Marked for Life* (SPCK, 1979), p. 74.
4   Gregory of Nyssa, *Cantica Cantic*, Homily 5.
5   Jamie Buckingham, *A Way Through the Wilderness* (Kingsway, 1983), p. 140.
6   Rowan Williams, *Resurrection* (Darton, Longman and Todd, 1982), pp. 34, 90.
7   Philip Seddon, *Darkness*, Grove Spirituality Series 5 (Grove Booklets, 1983), p. 20.
8   François Malaval, *A Simple Method of Raising the Soul to Contemplation* Second Treatise, Dialogue xii (J. and M. Dent, 1931), p. 253.
9   Anonymous, *The Cloud of Unknowing* (Burns and Oates, 1924), p. 11.
10   ibid., p. 24.
11   Source unknown.
12   St Bernard, *Liber de diligendo deo* xi 33. Cited by Rowan Williams in *The Wound of Knowledge* (Darton, Longman and Todd, 1979), p. 112.
13   Cf. Gregory of Nyssa, *Life of Moses*, trans. A. J. Malherbe and E. Ferguson, Classics of Western Spirituality (Paulist Press, 1978), pp. 115, 116.
14   Apophatic theology taught that the light of God in the soul is sometimes experienced as darkness. Thus darkness and light, seeing and not seeing, knowing and unknowing may be identified.

In the strict sense the darkness is light. But by virtue of its transcendence it is described as darkness because it is invisible to those who seek to approach or see it through the activity of sense or intellect. It is a darkness that is, in truth, supremely bright; and in this 'dazzling darkness' divine things are given to believers. Now Christ is calling you to let go of your controlled thinking . . . and to surrender in deeper faith, hope and love to his indwelling presence, beyond any feeling you may have . . . Christ is calling you into deeper darkness, the darkening of your own rational knowledge, to enter into a new way of receiving the communication of himself in the 'luminous darkness' of faith.

(G. A. Maloney, *Singers of the New Song* [Ave Maria Press, 1985], p. 59).

15 Source unknown.
16 Carlo Carretto, *Letters from the Desert* (Darton, Longman and Todd, 1972), p. 137.
17 John Bunyan, *Grace Abounding to the Chief of Sinners*.
18 E. Herman, *The Meaning and Value of Mysticism* (James Clarke, 1915), p. 134.
19 Thomas Goodwin, *Three Several Ages of Christians in Faith and Obedience*. Works Vol. 8, p. 290.
20 E. Herman, *The Meaning and Value of Mysticism*, p. 134.
21 Miguel de Molinos, *A Spiritual Guide which Disentangles the Soul* (Methuen, 1907), book 3, chap 3: 18
22 Samuel Rutherford, *Letters of Samuel Rutherford* (Oliphant, Anderson and Ferrier, 1894), p. 423.
23 Source unknown. Reproduced in my own words from memory.

Chapter 10   'Into your hands'

1 Henri Nouwen, *Reaching Out* (Fount, 1980), pp. 117–118.
2 John White, *People in Prayer* (IVP, 1977), p. 155.
3 ibid., p. 156.
4 Maisie Spens, *Concerning Himself* (Hodder and Stoughton, 1937), p. 291.
5 ibid.
6 Minnie Louise Haskins, verse one of 'God Knows' from *The Desert* (Bristol, 1908).
7 Elizabeth Basset. Ian MacHorton's story is told in my own words, and is taken from 'Safer than a known way' Part iv 'The companion' of *An Anthology – Each in Prison* (SPCK).
8 'O Jesus I have promised to serve thee to the end', *The English Hymnal* (OUP, 1906), No 577.

Chapter 11 'Pray then like this'

1 Jerusalem Community Rule of Life, *A City Not Forsaken* (Darton, Longman and Todd, 1985), p. 10.
2 Amy Carmichael, *Thou Givest . . . They Gather* (Lutterworth Press, 1958), p. 44.
3 John Bunyan, *The Pilgrim's Progress* (Collins), pp. 205–206.
4 Jerusalem Community Rule of Life, *A City Not Forsaken*, p. 14.
5 Cited in Amy Carmichael, *Thou Gavest . . . They Gather*, p. 54.
6 David Watson. Originally written in a circular letter to friends just before his death, later reproduced (with permission) in *Fiat*, the journal of the Community of St Mary the Virgin.
7 Richard Baxter, 'He wants not friends that hath thy love', *The English Hymnal* (OUP, 1906), No 401.

Chapter 12 'Our Father in heaven'

1 Martin Luther, 'A Simple Way to Pray for a good friend', *Luther's Works* 43, pp. 198–200, cited in Roger Pooley and Philip Seddon, *The Lord of the Journey* (Collins, 1986), p. 218.
2 Carroll Simcox, *Living the Lord's Prayer* (Dacre Press, 1955), p. 14.
3 St Ambrose, in J. H. Strawley (ed), *St Ambrose on the Sacraments and on the Mysteries*, trans. T. Thompson (SPCK, 1950).
4 St John Climacus, *Ladder of Divine Ascent* 21 and 27, cited in Kallistos Ware, *The Power of the Name*, Fairacres Publication 43 (SLG Press, 1974), p. 11.
5 Bruce Marshall, *Father Malachy's Miracle* (Constable and Co), cited in Carroll Simcox, *Living the Lord's Prayer*, p. 34.
6 Kallistos Ware, *The Power of the Name*, pp. 25–26.
7 Charles Elliott, *Praying the Kingdom* (Darton, Longman and Todd, 1985), p. 1.
8 St Gregory of Vlastos. Source of prayer unknown.
9 Carroll Simcox, *Living the Lord's Prayer*, p. 78.
10 St Gregory of Vlastos. Source of prayer unknown.
11 John Howard Yoder, *The Politics of Jesus* (Wm. B. Eerdmans, 1972), p. 42.
12 Sister Kirsty, *The Choice* (Hodder and Stoughton, 1982), p. 183 citing James Forest, *Thomas Merton* (CTS, 1980), p. 97.
13 Mary A. Lathbury, 'Break Thou the bread of life', *Anglican Hymn Book* (Church Society, 1965), No 303.
14 Agnes Sanford, *The Healing Light* (Arthur James, 1972), p. 130.
15 Dietrich Bonhoeffer, *Life Together* (SCM Press, 1954), pp. 90–91.
16 John Howard Yoder, *The Politics of Jesus*, p. 67.

17 ibid.
18 Charles Elliott, *Praying the Kingdom* (Darton, Longman and Todd, 1985), p. 28.
19 ibid., p. 23.
20 Carroll Simcox, *Living the Lord's Prayer*, p. 72.

Chapter 13 'Watch and pray'

1 C. H. Dodd, *Parables of the Kingdom* (Fount, 1978), p. 27.
2 S. J. Stone, 'Weary of earth and laden with my sin', *The English Hymnal* (OUP, 1906), No 91.

BIOGRAPHICAL DICTIONARY OF AUTHORS

(contemp. = contemporary)

Allchin, A. M.	contemp.	Canon of Canterbury Cathedral; Warden of Sisters of the Love of God, Fairacres.
Ambrose of Milan	340–397	Bishop of Milan.
St Augustine	354–430	Bishop of Hippo.
Bassett, Lady Elizabeth	contemp.	Lady in Waiting to Queen Elizabeth, the Queen Mother, and second daughter of the 7th Earl of Dartmouth. Author of the anthologies *Love is my Meaning* and *The Bridge is Love*.
St Bernard	1090–1153	Abbot of Clairvaux.
Bloom, Anthony	contemp.	Metropolitan. Head of Russian Orthodox Church in Great Britain and Ireland.
Bonhoeffer, Dietrich	1906–1944	German Lutheran theologian executed by the Nazis. *Life Together* was written on the eve of World War II as a result of his experience as head of a seminary at Finkenwalde.
Boom, ten Corrie	c.1900–1980	Author of *The Hiding Place* telling of her work of sheltering Jews from the Nazis and her subsequent internment in a concentration camp.
Boulding, Dame Maria osb	contemp.	Nun of the Benedictine Community of Stanbrook Abbey.
Brakkenstein Community		Brakkenstein Community of Blessed Sacrament Fathers, Holland.

Buckingham, Jamie	contemp.	Leader of several pilgrimages through the wilderness of Sinai. Author of *Risky Living* and *Where Eagles Soar*.
Buber, Martin	1878–1965	Jewish thinker and mystic. Author of *I and Thou*; *Between Man and Man?*; *The Eclipse of God*.
Bunyan, John	1628–1688	Baptist preacher in Bedford. Author of the allegory *Pilgrim's Progress* and his autobiography *Grace Abounding*.
Caretto, Carlo	contemp.	A Little Brother of Jesus – the Order inspired by Charles de Foucauld.
Carmichael, Amy	1867–1951	First Keswick missionary and founder of the Dohnavur Fellowship.
de Caussade, Jean Pierre	1675–1751	Jesuit. Did much to rehabilitate mysticism at a time when it was suffering in the wake of the condemnation of Quietism.
Climacus, St John	*c*.579–*c*.649	Abbot of Sinai.
Cloud of Unknowing	Fourth century	Spiritual classic by anonymous author.
Coggan, Donald	contemp.	His Grace, the former Archbishop of Canterbury.
Cooke, Frank	contemp.	Minister of Andover Baptist Church, Hants and Director of Purley and Andover Christian Trust.
Dodd, C. H.	contemp.	Emeritus Professor of Divinity, Cambridge.
Dumitriu, Petru	contemp.	Rumanian poet and novelist. Finding himself unable to reconcile his conscience with the tyranny of the Communist Party, he fled with his wife to the West in February 1960.
Ecclestone, Alan	contemp.	Anglican Priest, contributor to *Spirituality Today* and author of *A Staircase for Silence*; *The Night Sky of the Lord* and *Yes to God*.

El-Meskeen, Fr Matta	contemp.	Abbot of Macarius Monastery, Cairo.
Eichrodt, Walter	contemp.	Theologian and one-time Professor in University of Basle.
Elphinstone, The Hon. Andrew		One-time ADC to the Viceroy of India and former Rector of Worplesdon, Surrey. He died before his book was completed but the final revision was made by Professor Gordon Dunstan.
Elliott, Charles	contemp.	Former Director of Christian Aid and a leading authority on development economics.
Finley, James	contemp.	Former Novice of Gethsemani Monastery, Kentucky, when Thomas Merton was Novice Guardian.
Foster, Richard	contemp.	Associate Professor at the Friends' University, Wichita, Kansas. Author of *Celebration of Discipline*; *Freedom of Simplicity* and *Money, Sex and Power*.
Goodwin, Thomas	1600–1679	Noncomformist leader whose writings provide typical exposition of Puritan spirituality.
Goudge, Elizabeth	1900–1982	English novelist.
Grant, Patrick	contemp.	Professor of English at University of Victoria, Canada.
Gregory of Nyssa	c.330–395	Bishop of Nyssa from c.371. Brother of Basil of Caesarea. Thinker and theologian of great originality. Leading exponent of the Apophatic Tradition.
Gregory of Vlastos		Details unknown.
Guyon, Madame	1648–1717	French Quietist author.
Hammarskjöld, Dag	1905–1961	Former General Secretary of United Nations. Swedish and a mystic. Killed in an air crash over the Congo.

Haskins, Minnie Louise	1875–1954	Lecturer in Social Sciences, London School of Economics and author of *The Desert* an anthology of poetry including *God Knows* immortalised by King George VI.
Herman, E.	Early twentieth century	Author of *Creative Prayer* and *The Meaning and Value of Mysticism*. Mrs Herman established herself as a writer of spiritual penetration and power in the earlier part of this century.
Hughes, Gerard	contemp.	Jesuit author of *In Search of a Way* and *God of Surprises*.
Ignatius of Loyola	1491–1556	Founder of the Society of Jesus (Jesuits) who introduced the well known *Spiritual Exercises*.
Isaac of Stella	*c*.1100–*c*.1169	Cistercian Abbot of the *Île d'Étoile* near Poitiers.
Israel, Martin	contemp.	The Rev. Dr Martin Israel lectures in pathology at the University of London, is author of many books on spirituality and healing and a much sought-after Spiritual Director.
Jefferies, Richard	1848–1887	Countryman, mystic and author.
Jeremias, Joachim	contemp.	German theologian, scholar and one-time professor at Göttingen.
Johnston, William	contemp.	Jesuit. Author of many books exploring the boundaries between Christian and Eastern mysticism.
Julian, Mother, of Norwich	*c*.1342–1420	English anchoress and mystic. Writer of *Revelations of Divine Love*.
Jung, C. G.	1875–1961	Famous analytical psychologist whose contributions to religious psychology exceed that of any other writer in this century.

Kirsty, Sister	contemp.	The pseudonym of a csmv Sister, author of *The Choice* the story of the early years of formation in a Religious Community.
Lewis, C. S.	1898–1963	One-time Fellow and tutor, Magdalen College, Oxford. Christian scholar, allegorist and brilliant writer on a wide variety of subjects.
Lull, Ramon	1233–1315	Lay missionary and philosopher of Majorca. Author of *The Book of the Lover and the Beloved*.
Luther, Martin	1483–1546	One-time Monk. Theologian, musician and reformer.
Malaval, François	1672–after 1703	Contemporary of Brother Lawrence; saw the rise and fall of Madame Guyon and the 'new mystics'. Blind from the age of 9 months, he became a leading scholar of his day, and a mystic.
Mary Clare, Mother slg	contemp.	Former Reverend Mother of the Community of Sisters of the Love of God, Fairacres.
Merton, Thomas	1915–1968	Cistercian Monk of the Strict Order, Gethsemani Abbey, Kentucky. Prolific writer on spirituality. Killed in an accident, Bangkok, 1968.
Molinos, Miguel de	1640–1697	Spanish Quietist.
Moorhouse, Geoffrey	contemp.	Writer. Author of *Against All Reason*; *The Christians* and *The Fearful Void*.
Murray, Andrew	1828–1917	South African minister of the Dutch Reformed Church.
Nouwen, Henri	contemp.	
Ortiz, Juan Carlos	contemp.	Evangelist from Buenos Aires, now in USA, with wide teaching and preaching ministry.
Pullinger, Jackie	contemp.	Missionary extraordinary in Hong Kong with special ministry to

the Walled City and its drug
addicts.

Quoist, Michel	contemp.	French Roman Catholic Priest – much involved in the worker priest movement and social action. Now spends much time in giving retreats.
Rilke, Rainer M.	1875–1926	German poet who greatly influenced modern European literature.
Robinson, Wendy	contemp.	Counsellor, psychiatric social worker and author, living in Oxford.
Rolle, Richard	1295–1349	English mystic and hermit of Hampole.
Runcorn, David	contemp.	Chaplain of Lee Abbey Fellowship.
Rutherford, Samuel	1600–1661	Scottish Presbyterian Divine; imprisoned for conscience, during which time he wrote many pastoral letters which have been preserved.
Ruysbroeck, John Van	1293–1381	Flemish Mystic. Formed Community of Canons Regular and became Prior.
Sanders, Oswald	contemp.	American evangelical preacher and writer.
Sanford, Agnes	1897–1982	Wife of Episcopalian priest; exercised a remarkable healing ministry. Author of a number of books.
Seddon, Philip	contemp.	Central Staff of Professors, Selly Oak Colleges, Birmingham.
Simcox, Carroll	contemp.	Author of *Living the Creed* and *The Lord's Prayer*.
St Seraphim of Zarov	1759–1833	Saint, hermit, mystic of Russian Orthodox Church who was greatly used as a Counsellor and Spiritual Director.
Teilhard, de Chardin	1881–1955	Jesuit priest and paleontologist.
Temple, William	1881–1944	Former Archbishop of Canterbury.

Teresa of Avila	1515–1582	Spanish Carmelite nun and mystic.
St Thierry, William of	1085–1148	Cistercian monk, theologian and mystical writer. Friend of St Bernard.
Tozer, Aidan W.	1897–1963	American minister. With no teacher but the Holy Spirit and good books, he became a theologian and scholar. Evangelical mystics were his favourite study.
Underhill, Evelyn	1875–1941	Anglican scholar, mystic, retreat giver and prolific author.
Vanstone, W. H.	contemp.	Canon Residentiary of Chester Cathedral and member of the Doctrine Commission of the Church of England.
Verney, Stephen	contemp.	Former Bishop Suffragan of Repton.
Waal, Esther de	contemp.	Wife of former Dean of Canterbury. Author of *Seeking God*.
Ware, Kallistos	contemp.	Bishop of Diokleia and Spalding lecturer in Eastern Orthodox Studies in University of Oxford, member of the Monastic Brotherhood of St John the Theologian, Patmos.
Watson, David	1933–1984	Anglican evangelical priest with notable ministry at St Michael by le Belfrey, York, and in University Missions. Author of a number of books.
Whichcote, Benjamin	1609–1683	Provost of King's College, Cambridge.
White, John	contemp.	Psychiatrist. Formerly Associate Professor of Psychiatry at University of Manitoba. Has worked with International Fellowship of Evangelical Students.
Whittier, John Greenleaf	1807–1892	Famous hymn writer.

Wilkins, Eithne	contemp.	At the time of writing *The Rose Garden Game*, 1969, she was Reader in Modern German Literature at University of Reading.
Williams, Maurice	contemp.	Minister of Amersham Free Church.
Williams, Rowan	contemp.	Lady Margaret Professor of Divinity, Oxford. Author of *The Wound of Knowledge*; *The Truce of God*; *Resurrection*.
Yoder, John Howard	contemp.	Associate Director of the Institute of Mennonite Studies and President of Goshen Biblical Seminary.
Zernov, Militza, Dr	contemp.	Wife of Dr Nicolas Zernov. Authority on iconography.
Zernov, Nicolas, Dr	1898–1980	Founder of the Anglican-Orthodox Fellowship of St Alban & St Sergius and first editor of its journal *Sobornost*; founder of the House of St Gregory and St Macrina, Oxford – an ecumenical centre. Lecturer of Oxford University.

SCRIPTURE INDEX

Apocrypha

AUTHOR INDEX

SUBJECT INDEX